Slovenia

Slovenia

BY TAMRA ORR

Enchantment of the World
Second Series

Children's Press®

A Division of Scholastic Inc.

NEW YORK   TORONTO   LONDON   AUCKLAND   SYDNEY
MEXICO CITY   NEW DELHI   HONG KONG
DANBURY, CONNECTICUT

Frontispiece: Ljubljanica River

Consultant: Dr. Amy J. Johnson, Assistant Professor of History, Berry College, Mount Berry, GA

Please note: All statistics are as up-to-date as possible at the time of publication.

Book production by Herman Adler Design

Library of Congress Cataloging-in-Publication Data

Orr, Tamra.
  Slovenia / by Tamra Orr.
    p. cm. — (Enchantment of the world. Second series)
Includes bibliographical references and index.
    ISBN 0-516-24249-0
1. Slovenia—Juvenile literature. [1. Slovenia.] I. Title. II. Series.
    DR1360.O77 2003
    949.73—dc22   2003015253

CHILDREN'S PRESS and associated logos are trademarks and or registered
trademarks of Scholastic Library Publishing. SCHOLASTIC and associated logos
are trademarks and or registered trademarks of Scholastic Inc.
1 2 3 4 5 6 7 8 9 10 R 13 12 11 10 09 08 07 06 05 04

Slovenia

Contents

Cover photo:
Lake Bled church
and castle

Kranj

Slovene women

A Small but Mighty Country

F INDING SLOVENIA ON A MAP MIGHT PROVE RATHER CHALlenging for many people—especially if the map was drawn before 1991. First of all, the country did not exist before June 25, 1991; it had not yet gained its independence from Yugoslavia. Secondly, many times this small country is confused with Slovakia, a small country that lies between Hungary and Poland. Despite its newness and small size, Slovenia is a country that is not only beautiful, but also economically stable and rich with history.

Opposite: **Slovenia lies in the heart of Europe where the Alps and the Mediterranean meet.**

Geopolitical map of Slovenia

Slovenia is a very pleasurable place to visit. Because of its location, it is often associated with the Balkans, a large region that includes Serbia, Bosnia and Herzegovina, and Albania.

Unfortunately, Slovenia has also been mistakenly associated with the bitter problems and violence in the neighboring countries of Croatia and Bosnia and Herzegovina. In truth, the Slovenes had no part in the fighting and terrorism that filled those countries. Instead, it has remained at peace. It has remained a place where its citizens could live and tourists could visit in complete safety. While the number of tourists fell during the 1998–1999 war in nearby Kosovo in southern Serbia, it is on the way back up again as people from all over the world discover this charming country just off the Adriatic Sea.

Enjoying the Beauty

Tourists from many other countries travel to Slovenia to enjoy its many attractions. From December to March, thousands of winter sports lovers come to Slovenia with their equipment in tow. They come prepared to enjoy their favorite hobbies—skiing (both downhill and cross-country) and snowboarding. The mountains and thick snow of this region are just what they need. While the mountains here are smaller than those found at other European resorts, they are surrounded by beautiful scenery. Plus, the resorts in Slovenia offer lower prices to tourists on budgets. Most of the resorts offer everything from snowboard schools to equipment rentals and a variety of restaurants. Kanin, the country's highest ski resort, offers

Slovenes have countless
well-marked mountain and
hiking trails at their disposal.

incredible views of area landmarks such as Mount Triglav (the country's highest mountain) and the Julian Alps, as well as a far-off view of the Adriatic Sea. Winter sports enthusiasts who would prefer to just watch also come to Slovenia to attend the international ski-jumping and ski-flying competitions held at Planica (the largest downhill slope). Slovenes are found on the slopes quite often; skiing is their favorite sport.

Mountain and rock climbers head for the peaks and rock faces of the Julian Alps or for the challenging north face of Triglav. Tourists who would rather stay closer to the ground can take advantage of the hiking and mountain walking trails throughout the country. Slovenes like to hike almost as much as they like to ski, and visitors often learn the most about the locals by chatting with them on the more than 4,350 miles (7,000 kilometers) of trails available. In 2000, Slovenia joined with seven other countries (France, Italy, Monaco, Switzerland, Germany, Austria, and Liechtenstein) to form the Via Alpina, a 341-day long-distance trail that will follow the complete arc of the Alps. It was launched in the summer of 2002 and will most likely attract hikers from all over the world.

In addition to this, people also travel to Slovenia to do other outdoor activities, ranging from kayaking and cycling to caving and fishing. River sports like white-water rafting and canoeing take place on any of Slovenia's half-dozen rivers that have fast-running water, including the popular Soča River in Primorska.

Dedicated cyclists who like to pedal their way through trails and mountains appreciate Slovenia. Mountain bikes can

Outdoor activities in Slovenia include mountain biking through the Alpine region.

be rented in several places throughout the country and riders can make their way along streets, through mountain trails and forests, and even on a downhill racecourse for the especially brave.

Slovenia is full of caves—almost 7,000 have already been identified and explored. Tourists are allowed to walk their way through two dozen of them, while native Slovenes and others

Cavers explore Bestazovca Cave, one of more than 7,000 caves in Slovenia.

often try rafting through some of the caves. Thanks to the many waterways found throughout the country, fishing is also a popular pastime. Mountain streams offer trout, while lakes and rivers feature pike, perch, and carp. In fact, the Soča River is considered to be one of the best trout-fishing rivers in all of Europe.

Opposite: **Bled Castle, once the summer home of Yugoslav royalty, is first mentioned in a document dating from the year 1004 and is preparing for its first millennial anniversary.**

Enjoying the History

Slovenia was once called the "country of castles," and boasted more than 1,000 scattered across the area. While the march of modern building destroyed most of them, some still remain, giving everyone a true glimpse into the distant past. The most unusual castle open to tourists is Bled Castle. Balanced on the top of a steep cliff over 328 feet (100 meters) high, it overlooks a lake. Complete with towers, ramparts, and even a moat, Bled Castle dates back to the eleventh century, and includes a museum collection that dates as far back in time to the Bronze Age (2300 B.C.–1050 B.C.). Armor and weapons can be found there, along with a sixteenth century chapel and early Slav burial pits.

Along with castles, Slovenia features many different churches. There is the beautiful Church of Saint John the Baptist at Bohinj to the Church of the Assumption on Bled Island, the country's only actual island, which can only be reached by rowboat or a ride on a gondola. Many of the churches are open for tourists to visit, including the

In front of the Ursuline Church of the Holy Trinity is the Holy Trinity column, built in gratitude that the town was spared from the plague.

Baroque-style Ursuline Church of the Holy Trinity in the capital city of Ljubljana, where people can see a multicolored altar made out of African marble.

Along with these historical sites, Slovenia has a number of museums throughout the country. The Saltworks Museum in Sečovlje, a historical site demonstrating how salt was once collected, is quite unusual. The Beekeeping Museum in Radovljica reflects the country's enduring interest in bees and harvesting honey. The Slovenian Ethnographic Museum, located in the capital city, houses the most impressive collections of Slovenian art, culture, and crafts. Ljubljana contains quite a few other rather unusual museums, including a brewery museum, a railway museum, and a tobacco museum.

Enjoying the Culture

Although the country is relatively new, Slovenia has still managed to make a big splash in the area of culture. Music is important to the Slovenes, and rock bands like Laibach not only entertain their fans but also present contemporary political messages to share and inspire the people. Folk music continues to be a favorite, and the Institute of Music and National Manuscripts is in charge of collecting and protecting the traditional wedding marches, children's songs, and stories that have been set to music.

Dance is also important to this region. Since the turn of the twentieth century, ballet has been popular, and the Ljubljana Ballet goes on national tours, as well as performing locally. Folk dancing, circle dancing, and polkas are still favorite forms of entertainment.

Slovenes have been fond of poetry for a long time. One of their most beloved writers is the Romantic poet France Prešeren. His life was full of hardships and disappointments, but he is now revered, and his image can be found throughout the country in statues, on stamps, and on currency. His lyrical, epic poems spoke of brotherhood and national pride. Slovene literature continues to grow, and the nation appreciates and supports a number of poets.

Whether a person wishes to enjoy Slovenia as a possible vacation spot, or simply a place to read and learn about, there certainly is enough there to entertain and educate. It is a country that has only been able to claim its political independence for little more than a decade, but it is rich in beauty, history, and a culture going back hundreds of years.

Frigid Alps to Underground Caverns

SLOVENIA SITS AT THE CROSSROADS OF CENTRAL EUROPE, the Mediterranean, and the Balkans. To the west is Italy; to the east is much of Croatia, as well as a small portion of Hungary. Austria borders the country in the north. It is not a large country; at slightly under 8,000 square miles (20,720 sq km), it is just a little bit smaller than New Jersey. Yet, on this miniscule amount of land, it manages to pack in everything from beautiful mountains that rise up in the air thousands of feet to magnificent underground limestone caverns, to endless rolling hills of vineyards.

The first thing that strikes anyone looking at Slovenia is just how overwhelmingly green it is! Slightly over half of the country is forested, making it the third most wooded country in all of Europe. Almost the entire country is blanketed in forests, orchards, vineyards, meadows, and fields. The areas that aren't green are usually host to a number of mountain ranges, many of which rise up over 8,000 feet (2,440 m) high. In fact, almost 90 percent of the entire country is about 1,000 feet (305 m) above sea level.

Opposite: **Much of Slovenia is mountainous beginning with the Julian Alps in the northwest and continuing with the main Alpine chain along the border with Austria.**

The Regions of Slovenia

Geographically, Slovenia can be divided into six main regions, each with its own unique elements and having either a Mediterranean, Continental, or Alpine climate. The Alpine

Slovenia's Geographic Features

Highest Peak: Mount Triglav, 9,400 feet (2,864 m)

Lowest Elevation: sea level at the coast

Greatest Distance North to South: 100 miles (161 km)

Greatest Distance East to West: 155 miles (249 km)

Largest Permanent Lake: Lake Bohinj, 2.8 miles (4.5 km) long

Longest River: Sava River, 136 miles (219 km)

Largest Protected Natural Area: Triglav National Park, 323.6 square miles (838 sq km)

Highest Waterfall: Cedca, 427 feet (130. m) high

Greatest Precipitation: 117 inches (297 cm) a year in the northwest regions

Highest Temperatures: over 100°F (37.7°C) in the northeast regions

Largest City: Ljubljana, the capital, 330,000 people

Mount Triglav is the highest peak in the Julian Alps and is at the center of the Triglav National Park.

region of the country is in the north and northwest section of the country. It includes different mountain ranges: the Julian Alps, the Karawanken Alps, and the Kamnik-Savinja Alps.

The Julian Alps include Slovenia's most famous landmark, Mount Triglav, the country's highest peak, reaching 9,400 feet (2,864 m). This area is very cold with lots of snow in the winter and heavy rains in the summer. This region has the most precipitation in the country, often averaging about 117 inches (297 centimeters) a year, half of that in snow. These mountains seem to call to the world's climbers and

The Pre-Alpine hills, found to the south and east of Slovenia's Alps.

skiers, and are a big tourist attraction in the winter months, despite the frigid weather.

On the southern and eastern sides of the Alps is a region called the Pre-Alpine Hills. While still mountainous, this area also includes limestone and magnesium-rich dolomite peaks. This area also has very cold winters with warm and pleasant summers.

The Dinaric Karst region consists of caverns, underground tunnels, and sink holes (pictured).

The Dinaric Karst region is located south/southwest of the capital city, Ljubljana, and close to the Italian border. The word karst refers to the limestone regions of underground rivers, gorges, and caves below the hills that are found throughout the region. This area mainly consists of plateaus and enjoys a more Continental climate of hot summers and cold winters.

The Slovenian littoral, or Adriatic coastal region, is in the southwest portion of the country. With only about 30 miles (48 km) of coastline, Slovenia is nevertheless considered to be a maritime (sea) country. This area has a definite

Mediterranean climate of hot, dry summers (sometimes reaching more than 100°Fahrenheit [37.7° Celsius]) and mild winters.

The east and northeast portion of Slovenia is called the Pannonian plain. It is primarily made up of hills and extensive areas of gravel and clay. The eastern areas have the least rainfall during the year, averaging about 31 or 32 inches (79 or 81 cm) annually. Despite this, the Pannonian plain is full of fertile farmland. Many of the country's vineyards are found here, thanks to a great deal of natural springs in the area. Merging into the plains is the region called the lowlands. The lowlands also in the east and northeast region, with a dry, warm climate. This area makes up about one-fifth of the entire country.

The fertile Slovenian countryside in the Pannonian plain is often referred to as the "green sea."

Looking at Slovenia's Cities

The second-largest city in Slovenia, Maribor, has a population of 135,863. It is located in the northeast part of the country and is considered to be the strongest industrial city with chemical, engineering, and electrical companies throughout. It sits on the border between the Pohorje Mountain range and the flatlands in the southeast. This gives it the best of both worlds—the skiing and climate from the mountains and the food production of the flatlands. The hills in the north are the perfect place for growing grapevines for making the country's excellent wines. In fact, this city claims the oldest grapevine in the whole world—reputed to be over 400 years old. Each year, its grapes are gathered in a ceremony and then made into a special wine.

The bustling city of Kranj (below), with a population of 52,360, has enough attractions for everyone. The transcontinental railroad that runs from London, England to Istanbul, Turkey comes through here, as do

the major highways going from Western to Eastern Europe. It has a history of being the seat of government and is the city where the nationally beloved poet France Prešeren worked and died. The University of Maribor's School of Organizational Sciences is found here, along with some of the most outstanding sports training facilities in the world.

Celje sits close to the middle of Slovenia and is often referred to as the heart of the country. The population of Celje is 50,239. The city has the advantage that almost all of the traffic from neighboring cities flows to it, making it a truly international commercial center. Despite this, the city still has signs of its long history as seen in the ancient castle walls that run throughout. Although Celje is small enough to cover in one long stroll, most tourists spend more time in the city discovering its old world charm. Thanks to its rich history, it is considered a town with real soul and spirit.

It features something for all visitors, from museums and galleries to concerts and exotic restaurants.

In the extreme southwest corner of Slovenia is the port city of Koper (above). With a population of 47,983, it is a bustling city dedicated to being one of the most technically advanced ports in the world. It sits at the junction of international trade routes and links the commercial centers in Central and Eastern Europe with Mediterranean countries and the Far East. It features up-to-date loading, transport, and storage systems for the many ships that dock there.

Nova Gorica, which sits right next to the Italian border, has a population of 43,249. A relatively new city compared with others, it was built in 1948, after World War II. Today it is considered the cultural and economic center for western Slovenia, and tourists enjoy the new theater built there, as well as the numerous rose gardens.

The town of Kostanjevica is built on an island in the middle of the Krka River.

Besides being extraordinarily green, Slovenia is also a very wet country. It has over 16,000 miles (25,744 km) of permanent waterways, plus thousands of mineral and thermal springs, waterfalls, gorges, and both natural and artificial lakes.

At 30 miles (48 km) long, the country's coast may be relatively small in size, but it is huge in importance to the Slovenes. It gives the people access to the world's oceans and its various imports and exports. Its warmer climate brings tourists by the thousands for winter sports or fun in the sun.

Slovenia also has a huge network of rivers running through it. The Sava River is the country's central and longest river. Over its 136-mile (219-km) course, it flows through mountains and hills, and ends up in the lowlands. On the way it features waterfalls, gorges, and rapids. The Krka River is called the Beauty

Kayakers enjoy the beauty
and challenge of the alpine
Soča River.

of Dolenjska and it is almost 70 miles (113 km) long. It gets
warmer than most of the other rivers, attracting many swimmers
and fishermen.

Other rivers include the Kolpa, whose rapids attract the
most daring canoeists; the Drava, which features dams that
help generate electrical energy; and the Soča, considered to be
one of the most beautiful Alpine rivers. Its milky-blue color,
boulders, waterfalls, and river terraces amaze and awe locals
and tourists alike.

Lake Bohinj is located in Triglav National Park and is the largest glacier lake in Slovenia.

Lakes are much more rare in Slovenia than rivers, but just as appreciated. Natural lakes are primarily found in the Alpine region and the deepest and largest one is Lake Bohinj, located in a valley between the summits of Vogel and Prsivec Mountains. It is more than 1 square mile (2.6 sq km) in surface area and up to 148 feet (45 m) deep, but few swimmers are hardy enough to handle its chilly temperatures, which range from a nippy 47°F to 63°F (8.3°C to 17.2°C). Tourists are usually much happier spending time at the mile-square Lake Bled whose water can reach over 70°F (21.1°C) in the summer months. Lake Bled offers an island and a castle, too.

Slovenia has breathtaking waterfalls—more than 250 of them. They change with the seasons, from raging torrents during the spring rains to mere trickles in the hottest part of summer to breathtaking frozen sheets of ice in the winter. The Boka waterfall near the city of Bovec in the Upper Soča valley is one of the most amazing falls, dropping almost 350 feet (107 m) straight down during the spring, when the snows of the Kanin Plateau above it are melting.

Going Underground

Some of the most dramatic parts of Slovenia are actually found underground. With 6,700 karstic caves already explored and identified, there are just as many that have not yet been discovered. These caverns make up an incredible labyrinth of subterranean (underground) rivers,

Water runoff is quite heavy in the mountains of Slovenia, creating more than 250 waterfalls.

tunnels, and, of course, stalagmites (cone-shaped deposits on a cave floor) and stalactites (icicle-shaped formations hanging from cave roofs). The most famous of the caves is the Postojna Cave. Over millions of years, waters rich in calcium carbonate created this cave, which is over 12 miles (19 km) long. The second most popular cavern system is the Škocjan caves near Divaca in the southwest. Formed by the Reka

Visitors cross the Hanke Bridge in Škocjan Cave.

The Pollution Problem

Like many other areas of the world, Slovenia battles with air and water pollution. The Sava, Mura, and lower Savinja Rivers are polluted with domestic and industrial waste, while coastal waters have been showing signs of heavy metals and toxic chemicals.

The continual emission of nitrogen oxides from all of the vehicles on the highways of Slovenia are also damaging the pine forests, as well as many of the outdoor sculptures and buildings in the bigger cities. Some Slovenian cities burn coal for power stations or heating plants and the sulfur dioxide from the process is polluting the air.

Fortunately, the country is not ignoring these problems. Between 1985 and 1995, thanks to the introduction of gas heating and consumer education, sulfur dioxide emissions were cut in half and nitrogen oxide omissions were reduced by 20 percent. Water pollution is being reduced by setting up water-purifying plants and by close monitoring of how industries dispose of their waste. In 1999 the country established a National Environmental Protection Program to continue efforts to reduce pollution.

River, it features many wild trails and formations. It is so magnificent that it is listed on the United Nations Educational, Scientific and Cultural Organization's (UNESCO) List of World Heritage sites.

Earthquakes!

The year 1998 was very rough for the Slovenes. On April 12, the northwest corner of the country was hit with an earthquake measuring 5.6 on the Richter scale. Near the Slovenian-Austrian border, it reached closer to 8.0. Although there were no reported deaths, more than 700 people were left homeless due to landslides, and more than 300 buildings were either destroyed or damaged enough to be unfit for use. The next few days brought more than 150 aftershocks, measuring up to 3.3 on the Richter scale.

Four months later, in August, the country was hit by another earthquake in the Trebnje region, southeast of Ljubljana. This one registered 4.3 and damaged buildings in the area.

Then, when fall arrived, it brought heavy rains. The country's many rivers overflowed in November, causing massive flooding in Slovenia, along with other nearby nations. Thousands of residents were forced to abandon their homes, and routes between the capital and western regions were completely cut off. Power outages reached across the country. It took months to recover from all the damage that was done.

Animal and Plant Life

WITH SLOVENIA BEING SUCH A FERTILE COUNTRY, COVered in everything from trees to meadows to vineyards, it's easy to see why there is an abundance of plant and animal life found there. Slovenia is known for over 50,000 species of animals and almost 3,000 plant species.

Opposite: **The mouflon, a rare breed of sheep, is home in the forests of Slovenia.**

Animals Common and Rare

Many of the animals found in Slovenia are common ones: deer, boars, bears, wolves, squirrels, foxes, badgers, and wildcats. However, some are more unusual. For example, the

Deer are found in abundance in Slovenia.

chamois, a type of horned goat-like antelope, lives here, as well as the moor tortoise and cave hedgehog. The lynx, a gray-brown member of the cat family with thick fur and ear tufts, was reintroduced into the area in 1973, and recently, the ibex, a type of mountain goat that has two long horns that bend backward, has been reintroduced to the environment. Previously, it had been extinct in Slovenia for three centuries. The only animals from Slovenia on the endangered list are seven species of bats.

Because of the unique mixtures of landscapes and climates, bird life is extensive in this country, including everything from grouse, eagles, and owls. Over 375 different bird species have been identified in Slovenia so far. They are drawn to areas like the Sečovlje saltpans and the Ljubljana Marshes. The various lakes and fishponds attract migrating species like ducks and herons, while the forests and the Alpine regions are home to

Grey herons are seen among the marshes and ponds in Slovenia.

The Famous Lipizzaners

A small village near the Italian border is the home of one of the most famous horses in the world—the white Lipizzaners. The Lipica Stud Farm near the city of Sezana has been there for more than 400 years. Austrian archduke Charles II, son of Ferdinand I, established it in 1580. He was quite particular about his horses and wanted a special place where his favorite— the elegant white Lipizzaner—could be bred and trained for the Spanish Riding School in Vienna, Austria. The farm offers tours of the stables, antique coach rides, and children's pony rides. Today, about 200 of these horses are still bred for use in shows and for riding. Born gray or chestnut colored, they turn white between five and ten years old, when their hair loses pigment, or color.

several types of owls and woodpeckers. Quail and skylarks can be found in the lowlands. Birds consider Slovenia to be a wonderful place for breeding, nesting, and migrating. Up to 20,000 waterfowl spend the winter at the Drava River in Maribor. In the spring between 4,000 and 8,000 black terns fill the Maribor skies as they begin their migration.

Slovenia's mountain streams are often full of all kinds of fish, including several kinds of trout, and its lakes have pike, perch, and carp. The favorite place in the country for fishermen is the Soča River.

A Mysterious Rarity

What is pale pink, can live up to a century, and is only found in the Karst region of the Dinaric Range? In this case, the right answer is the *Proteus anguinus*. Nicknamed the "human fish" for the color of its skin, this is a very unusual creature. Its name derives from Proteus, a Greek god, shepherd of all sea creatures and *anguinus* refers to its snake-like shape. It is actually classified as an amphibian and is cousin to the newt. Some refer to it as a cave salamander. It's the only known cave amphibian in existence and the largest cave animal in the world, averaging about 11 inches (28 cm) long.

Unlike other amphibians that reach maturity and leave their water homes to live on land and breathe air, the *Proteus anguinus* never leaves the water. It lives a long time, reaching maturity only after 12 to 18 years and then going on to live up to 100 years. The creature has two pairs of legs, is almost completely blind, and has a highly developed sense of smell. With no natural enemies, the *Proteus anguinus* swims safely throughout the waters of the Dinaric karst regions between Slovenia and Herzegovina. It eats small underwater animals, insect larvae, and occasionally even comes up to grab a water animal on the surface. In captivity, however, it's a

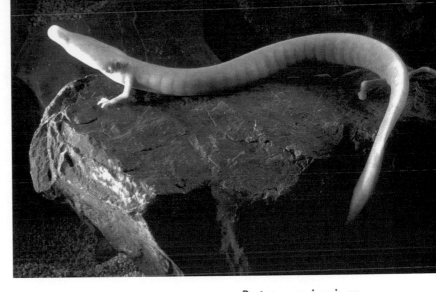

Proteus anguinus is an amphibian that has survived in the dark, underground caves of central Europe for several million years.

different story. Those that are kept in tanks to be observed can go incredible amounts of time without eating. In fact, in one recorded incident, a *Proteus anguinus* went twelve years without eating. When it finally died it was found that the creature's entire digestive system had disappeared!

In 1986, a new element to the mystery of the *Proteus anguinus* was discovered. An all-black species was found in Slovenia. At first, it was thought this was the usual *proteus* since the pale ones have been known to turn almost completely black if exposed to light for a prolonged time. However, this specimen was not only black, but had more defined eyes and a slightly different body shape, with a shorter head and stronger legs. Named *Proteus anguinus parkelj*, these animals are on the endangered list and are thought to live only in an area not much bigger than 50 miles (80.4 km). Because this "human fish" lives only in this limited area, it is considered to be a symbol of the country's fauna and natural heritage. It appears on Slovenia's currency and in the museums.

A Tour of Triglav National Park

One of the places in Slovenia that tourists and residents alike enjoy visiting is the 209,517-acre (83,807-hectare) Triglav National Park in Bled. Over 2 million people visit the park each year. Established in 1924 and enlarged in 1981, this is the place where all, but two, of the country's glacial lakes are located. Six waterfalls add to the park's beauty, along with a fascinating mixture of ravines, canyons, caves, rivers, and meadows. Of course, this is where the landmark Mount Triglav is located, from which the park gets its name. Other mountain peaks rise up in the clouds, and a number of visitors come just to climb them. Others come to hike through the meadows and forests.

The park is also home to a number of indigenous (native) flowers and animals of the area. The golden eagle and black grouse nest here, along with more unusual animals like the mouflon, a small, horned European sheep, and the marmot, a rodent with short legs and a bushy tail.

The rules are simple in the park—no littering, no picking the flowers, no starting fires, and no camping. There is an unusual tradition there too—visitors are expected to greet every person they pass. It makes the place even friendlier.

Flowers are everywhere throughout Slovenia. Seventy differ-ent types including Zois' bellflower and carniolan rose, are found nowhere else in the entire world. Zois' bellflower is often seen blossoming in the Alps toward the end of sum-mer. It was found over 200 years ago by botanist Karel Zois

Around 3,000 highland plants grow in Slovenia. Zois' bellflower was discovered more than 200 years ago and grows in the Julian Alps.

Slovenes in traditional dress pass out red carnations, Slovenia's national flower.

and named after him. Researchers believe that it has been around since before the Ice Age. One botanist wrote that it is "the daughter of the Slovene mountains."

The carniolan primrose is another Slovenian favorite. Like the bellflower, it was first discovered about 200 years ago and predates the Ice Age. It flowers in the spring in meadows and rocky fissures in the gorges. It has red-violet petal clusters and smooth, bright green leaves. Other local favorites include the Triglav rose, which is actually a pink cinquefoil, the blue Clusi gentian, yellow hawk's beard, Julian poppy, and carniolan lily. The national flower for Slovenia is the red carnation.

The Fine Art of Mushroom Hunting

Slovenes are avid mushroom hunters. In fact, the search for mushrooms is sometimes referred to as Slovenia's top national sport. People picked so many so often that finally laws had to be passed about how much any person could harvest on any given day. That way, no species would be hunted to extinction.

Mushroom hunting is an art as well as a sport in Slovenia, and there are many different species to choose from there. The information about each kind is handed down within families:

The Landmark Sečovlje Saltpans

On the border with Croatia is an usual sight—the abandoned saltpans of Sečovlje. Once the site of a thriving business, the 2.5-square-mile (6.5-sq-km) area sits quietly now, a mere ghost of the hustling, bustling industry it once was.

The saltpans are the site of where a salt lake used to be. For centuries salt was processed and shipped to other countries here. By using a system of canals, men would guide the water into ponds and using wind-powered pumps, evaporate the water from the salt. The salt would be drained, washed, ground, and sent out on barges to sell.

Today, the saltpans are abandoned as a business but are still home to over 150 species of birds that nest there, as well as 45 species of plants on Slovenia's Endangered Plant Species list. Visitors often stop by to look at the saltpans and to visit the Saltworks Museum located there, ranked in the top twelve by the European Museums Association. The exhibits there show the

lifestyles of the salt makers and their families. Tools, weights, baking utensils, and more are on display, along with a variety of texts and pictures. A special section of the museum has museum staff to help answer questions as well as to demonstrate how salt was made. Using the last wind-powered pump on the site, staff members share the process with tourists, and in the process make about 180 tons of salt each year in the traditional manner.

where they grow (some under just one kind of tree!); what months are the best times to pick a particular type (depending on the variety; some can be picked almost year round); and how they are best used. Some mushrooms are specifically for drying, others for frying. Some are put in sauces or stews while others are eaten raw or ground up into powder. Of course, everyone is also taught what mushrooms not to pick since there are quite a few deadly and poisonous ones out there as well.

At first glance, it often appears that all of Slovenia is covered in something green. Over half of the country is covered by trees. There are ten primeval (ancient) forests, some of which are too thick for humans to begin to walk through. The beech tree is the most common species, followed by different kinds of pines like the dwarf, Scotch, and Austrian. Spruce trees are found in many areas, along with the willow, alder, ash, and oak of the lowlands.

More than half of Slovenia is covered with forests. The trees in the forests change depending on the altitude in which they grow.

A good portion of Slovenia's other greenery is its almost 77,000 acres (31,185 ha) of vineyards. The area is perfect for growing wine grapes; it has the right climate and the Alps protect it from the harsh winter chill and the intense summer heat. The majority of the vineyards are found on the southern slopes of the Alps and the pre-Alpine hills below. A third of the vines being used in the vineyards are more than twenty years old.

According to archaeologists, viticulture, or wine making, has been practiced in the region for more than

Growing wine grapes in Slovenia began about 2,400 years ago. Today, about 53,373 acres (21,600 ha) of land is used for growing grapes.

2,400 years. Since the twelfth century, viticulture has continued to develop and has survived everything from the plague to aphid (slug) attacks. Today, the country produces between 21.1 and 23.8 million gallons (80 million and 90 million liters) of wine in the regions of Podravje, Posavje, and Primorje. Some are stored in wine cellars, while others are exported, sold at auction, or sold in local wine shops.

CHAPTER

FOUR

From Instability to Independence

Although the present country of Slovenia is only a little more than ten years old, the land itself still has a long history that reaches all the way back to 100,000 B.C. During its formation, it has changed hands, religions, leaders, and names a number of times.

Archaeologists have recently found tools made of bone in a cave near Orehek that date back between 60,000 and 100,000 years. From 1000 to 900 B.C., the people of this area lived by farming and raising cattle. In July 1995, Slovenian archaeologist Ivan Turk made a truly amazing discovery. In a cave located about 40 miles (64 km) from the country's capital, he found a 5-inch (13-cm) flute. It was made out of the femur, or large leg bone, of a bear and had four finger holes carved in it. Researchers were very excited to see it because Turk had just found the oldest known musical instrument in the world! This flute dates back to between 43,000 and 82,000 years ago, making its creator a Neanderthal, an extinct human species that lived during the late Pleistocene Epoch. Scientists and musicologists are still trying to understand what this means to what the world knows about Neanderthal society and the concept of music within a society.

Opposite: **Demonstrators show their support for Slovenia's independence in 1991.**

This flute, approximately 50,000 years old, was discovered in a cave in northwestern Slovenia in 1995.

Timeline of Dynasties

Celts	250 B.C.
Roman Empire	100 B.C.
Huns and Germanic tribes	476–670 A.D.
The Slavs and Carantanians; Bavarian-Frankish rule	745–1273
Habsburgs	1300–1918
Temporarily under France's control	1809–1814
Kingdom of the Serbs, Croats, and Slovenes	1918

Prior to the invading Germanic tribes, Attila and the Huns swept through, invading Slovenia and Italy.

Celtic tribes were among the first to live in Slovenia in approximately 250 B.C. The Romans moved into the area in 100 B.C. and divided it into several provinces, including Noricum, Upper and Lower Pannonia, and Histria. Many of the cities and rivers that are in Slovenia today got their names from this time period, including Bohinj and the Sava. The Romans stayed until the sixth century A.D., during which time Roman cities were formed. One of them was Emona (now Ljubljana). The arrival of the Romans also heralded the arrival of Christianity.

Centuries of Change

The next two centuries brought attacks by Attila and the Huns on their way to invade Italy. Following the Huns were other groups that held temporary control over the land, including the Germanic Ostrogoths and Langobards (or

Lombards). Finally, in the sixth century, the ancestors of those that would be today's Slovenes arrived and spread out through the river valleys and eastern Alps. As they continued to move out over the land, their numbers grew until they were almost 200,000 strong. Most were called Sclaveni. It wasn't until the late eighteenth century that the term Slovenians came into common use.

In the late seventh century, the Slavic people formed Carantania, but by the middle of the eighth century, the area came under Bavarian-Frankish rule and the concept of Christianity began to spread throughout the territory once again. By the beginning of the next century, Franks had replaced all of the Carantanian princes, and by the end of the century, a group called the Magyars came into the Pannonian area and cut the people

Holy Roman Empire, 1360

there off from the Slavs in the western portion. These Slavs, as well as those in the south, came together and formed an independent nation of Slovenes. They defeated the Magyars in 955, and the next several hundred years saw the land being divided into a number of border regions of the Holy Roman Empire.

The Brižinski Spomeniki, or Freising Manuscripts

Joseph Docen found an important historical document in 1806. Looking through a volume at the Freising Diocese, near Munich, Germany, he came across almost 170 pages of writing that he didn't recognize. It turned out to be three separate liturgies, or public worship forms; one was about sin and its consequences and the other two were directions on how to take confession with a priest. The amazing aspect to the documents, however, was that they dated back to between A.D. 972 and 1022. This made them the first-known Slovenian texts. Today the manuscripts are kept at the Bavarian State Archives in Munich and are considered Slovenia's most important documents.

A New Form of Slavery

From the late thirteenth century until just after the end of World War I, most of Slovenia's territory was controlled by the Habsburgs, an Austro-Hungarian family. They set the society up as a feudal system, where the Habsburgs owned all of the land and the peasants were allowed to live there for a fee, plus they had to work for the family and do whatever asked. It was, in effect, a type of slavery. The country began to develop economically as ironworks and mines were created, but the peasants were not happy about it. Between the years 1358 and 1848, the peasants revolted and rioted against the system more than one hundred times.

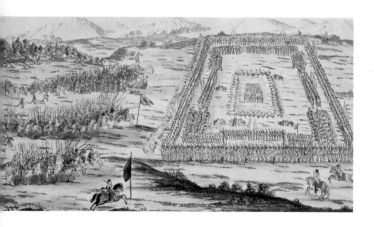

Ottoman expansion was great during the height of their power. As they moved into southeastern Europe, Austrian troops battled against the Turkish army to defend their land.

When the Ottoman Empire began to attack southeastern Europe, the Slovenes were forced to defend their feudal Habsburg lords. Thousands of peasants were either killed or taken prisoner, and this only made them angrier. Although the peasant revolts against the Habsburgs were violent—with the destruction of castles and execution of lords—the peasants weren't successful.

The Habsburgs retained control of the Slovene territory for four centuries. The only interruption came during the Napoleonic Wars when Napoleon Bonaparte attempted to cut off the Habsburg Empire from the Adriatic Coast. He took control of Slovenia and five other regions and named them the Illyrian Provinces.

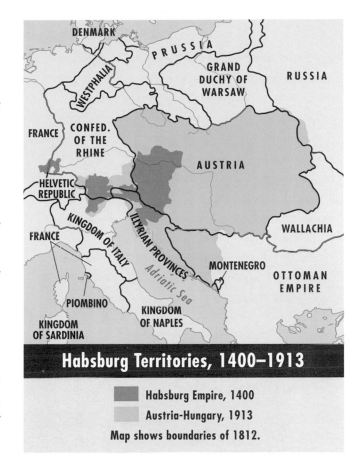

Habsburg Territories, 1400–1913

- ▮ Habsburg Empire, 1400
- ▮ Austria-Hungary, 1913

Map shows boundaries of 1812.

This was only temporary, however; by 1814 the Habsburgs were in control again and would be for another 100 years. But in the short time that Napoleon had power over the land, he made some significant changes. He instituted the use of the Slovene language in public schools and offices, and awoke the Slovenes to the possibility of national independence for the first time.

When Austrian rule returned after the defeat of Napoleon, Prince Klemens von Metternich immediately reinstated the feudal system that Napoleon had abolished. The Habsburgs

Mladina

In most societies, one of the first groups of people to speak out against something going on in their country are its writers. This is true in Slovenia also. A magazine called *Mladina*, which means "Youth," was established in Yugoslavia in 1943. It quickly got a reputation for being outspoken and very opinionated. In 1988 it went even further than that. It had become quite a mouth-piece for those wanting Slovenia to get its independence. It began attacking different elements in the Slovenian government. Three of the magazine's journalists, including the editor in chief, were arrested and given prison sentences for supposedly stealing military secrets. They appealed and were denied; but due to a legal technicality ended up never serving their sentences. In the meantime, all the publicity had made *Mladina* a very popular publication. Each issue sold out, with a circulation of more than 80,000.

During the ten-day war between emerging Slovenia and Yugoslavia, *Mladina* sent journalists in to cover both sides of the issue. They were the only publication to do so and what they saw not only made it into the magazine but into a book titled, *Ten Days of War for Slovenia*.

Mladina continues today and according to Slovenia Press, no politician is safe from their writers' sharp pencils because *Mladina* is not only a watchdog, but a watchdog that barks.

Kingdom of the Serbs, Croats, and Slovenes, 1919

also tried to repress any ideas of independence, but it was too late. The ideas had been planted and there was no stopping the Slovenes now. Writers all over Slovenia were supporting and discussing the ideals of freedom and their longing for unity among the people.

Moving Toward Independence

Following the end of World War I, the Austro-Hungarian Empire fell apart and so, in 1918, the Slovenes, Croats, and Serbs banded together. They declared themselves to be an independent state called the Kingdom of the Serbs,

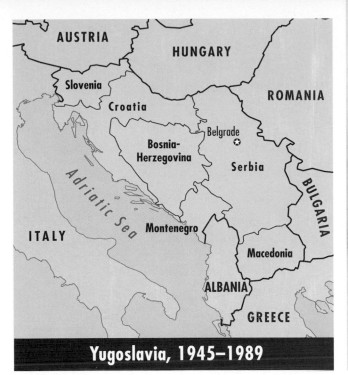

Yugoslavia, 1945–1989

During World War II, Germany occupied Slovenia. For most of the war, Slovenes fought a guerilla war, led by Marshall Tito, against the Nazis.

Croats, and Slovenes, including Serbia and Montenegro. The capital was in Zagreb. Together, they elected a prime minister and vice-premier. By this time, much of the original Slovenian territory was gone; the peace treaties signed in Paris after World War I had given away parts of the territory to Italy, Austria, and Hungary. This meant that many Slovenes were now living in other countries, and the loss of the land and the population was difficult for them.

The Kingdom of the Serbs, Croats, and Slovenes lasted until 1940, and although Slovenia was little more than a small province in it, it still benefited. Its culture and economy began to grow and progress was rapid. In 1929 the name of the state was changed to the Kingdom of Yugoslavia.

During World War II, much of Slovenia was taken by Germany, with Italy and Hungary grabbing smaller portions as well. The Kingdom of Yugoslavia began to fall apart, and in 1941, the Slovenes had had enough. They formed the Liberation Front of the Slovene Nation and armed themselves to fight back to keep their land. In 1945, Slovenia joined the newly formed Socialist Federal Republic of Yugoslavia, and by 1963, it was renamed the Socialist Republic of Slovenia. Throughout the 1950s and 1960s, Slovenia continued to grow and strengthen. The people focused more on creating a skilled workforce with organized labor, both of which worked together to build the confidence of the Slovenes. They began to truly feel that with these attributes, they were capable of reaching independence. With a high number of skilled workers and organized labor, gradually the Slovenes became more and more confident of their ability to reach independence.

By the late 1980s, Slovenia was struggling with its ties to Yugoslavia. The Slovenes felt that their connection to Yugoslavia was holding them back economically and culturally and they yearned to end the connection. Serbia appeared to be moving toward control of all the Yugoslav republics, and Slovenia didn't want that. In 1988 and 1989, the first political opposition parties were created and in April 1990, the first democratic elections were held in Slovenia. The Slovene declaration of independence

Supporters of the 1991 Slovenian Independence Movement hold the country's flag aloft.

came next on June 25, 1991. The following day, Yugoslavia sent in its army to try to stop the creation of the new state. However, the Yugoslav army met with unexpected resistance from Slovene police, the Territorial Defense Forces, and the population at large. In a matter of a few days, the Yugoslav army began to fall apart and

In June 1991 the Yugoslav army was called in by the central government to put a stop to the reform movement soon after Slovenia declared its independence.

within the week a truce was reached with the help of the leaders from the European Community (EC). The Yugoslav army withdrew and the ten day war was over. A total of sixty-six people lost their lives in the short-lived battle.

Slovenia had set a good example to its neighbors. In 1991, Macedonia declared its independence and the following year, Bosnia-Herzegovina did also, while Serbia and Montenegro came together to establish the Federal Republic of Yugoslavia. None of these declarations of freedom went as smoothly and quietly as Slovenia's had, unfortunately. In the mid-1990s, wars erupted involving Croatia, Serbia, and Bosnia and Herzegovina. Only a few years later, the war in Kosovo in Serbia erupted. Many thousands of lives were lost or destroyed before these other republics found their own independence. Throughout it all, Slovenia stayed out of the fighting and worked to strengthen their own country.

CHAPTER FIVE

A New Independence

W HEN SLOVENIA DECLARED ITS INDEPENDENCE JUST A
little over ten years ago, it had to set up an all-new government. The people chose to adopt a constitution in December
1991 that states, "Slovenia is a state of all its citizens and is
founded on the permanent and inalienable right of the
Slovenian nation to self-determination." Their government is
a parliamentary democracy, meaning that it is a government
where people can exercise their political power either directly
or, more often, through elected representatives.

Opposite: **A Slovenian flag is held by a statue of Slovene poet France Prešeren.**

Flag of Slovenia

The flag of Slovenia is made of three equal stripes of color: red on the bottom, white in the middle, and blue at the top. The colors date back to 1848, and are considered historical Slovene colors.

The coat of arms (right) was designed by Marko Pognacnik in 1991. He put a lot of meaning into every aspect of it. The three white peaks represent Mount Triglav, as well as the many other mountains of the region. The blue, wavy lines at the bottom represent the rivers and sea. The three golden stars were taken from the coat of arms of the counts of Celje. Pognacnik wanted this shield to represent the interconnected-ness of earth and sky and to include all the elements of fire, water, air, and earth.

President of the Republic

Born in Celje in 1950, Janez Drnovšek attended the University of Ljubljana's Faculty of Economics. In 1986 he completed his doctoral studies and went into banking. Three years later, Drnovšek, with a Ph.D. in Economics from the University of Maribor, was elected in the very first democratic elections to represent Slovenia in the collective presidency of the former Yugoslavia. During the year that he held this position, he worked to modernize the economy and promote human rights issues. He played a major role in liberating all the political prisoners being held in the former Yugoslavia.

As the country fought for its independence in 1991, Drnovšek was in charge of much of the discussions. When the Yugoslav People's Army invaded Slovenia in an attempt to stop their declaration of independence, Drnovšek led the negotiations that resulted in the withdrawal of forces and ending the war.

The following year, Drnovšek was elected prime minister of the Republic of Slovenia. He began focusing on improving the banking system and reorganizing different companies. He also helped Slovenia become a

member of important international institutions and associations like the United Nations, World Bank, and the North Atlantic Treaty Organization (NATO).

Drnovšek was elected to the position of prime minister four times. In addition, he has received a number of international awards. In December 2002, he was elected president and he continues to lecture at international establishments and universities.

The Executive and Legislative Branches

As set up within this system of government, the president of the republic represents the people and is commander of the armed forces. He is elected directly by secret ballot, and can serve a maximum of two five-year terms. President Janez Drnovšek is a popular Slovenian political leader who fought for the country's independence for years.

The prime minister is elected by the majority vote of the National Assembly deputies, after being nominated by the president. The prime minister is in charge of directing and leading the government and helps to maintain the causes and laws the government is working to enforce or change.

Anton Rop

In 2002, Anton Rop was elected prime minister of Slovenia. Born in 1960 in the capital city, Rop graduated from the Faculty of Economics and received the Prešeren Award for Students for his senior thesis. He continued his education and soon had a master's degree in economics.

From 1985 to 1992, Rop served as the assistant director of the Slovene Institute for Macroeconomic Analysis and Development. In that position, he worked on addressing many of Slovenia's economic issues. He published quite a few articles on the topics of investment and housing.

In 1993, Rop was appointed to the position of state secretary at the Ministry of Economic Relations and Development. He spent another three years as Minister of Labor, Family and Social Affairs, and in late 2002, he became Slovenia's new prime minister. His term will run until 2006.

Members of Slovenia's government in session.

Executive power in Slovenia comes from the prime minister, as well as his fifteen-member cabinet, called the Council of Ministers. The Council of Ministers consists of forty members from a wide mixture of backgrounds, including social, economic, professional, and local interest groups. Members are elected by the National Assembly for five years and they work in an advisory role, giving their counsel on matters within their areas of expertise.

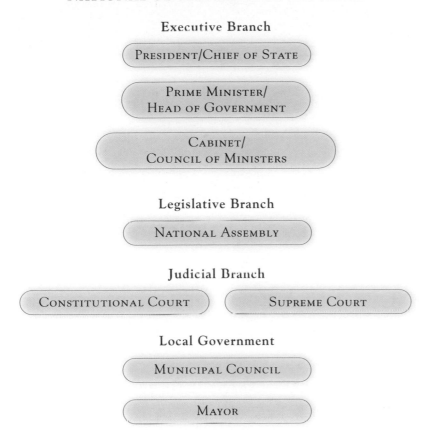

NATIONAL GOVERNMENT OF SLOVENIA

Executive Branch

President/Chief of State

Prime Minister/ Head of Government

Cabinet/ Council of Ministers

Legislative Branch

National Assembly

Judicial Branch

Constitutional Court

Supreme Court

Local Government

Municipal Council

Mayor

The Legislative Branch

The highest legislative body in Slovenia is called the National Assembly. It consists of ninety deputies who are elected directly by popular vote and serve four-year terms. One deputy is in charge of representing the Italian minority within Slovenia; another represents the Hungarians. The assembly passes laws and makes other important decisions, such as

Slovenia's National Assembly in session.

whether to ratify international agreements, to declare a state of war or emergency, and if the use of armed force is necessary.

In the National Assembly elections of October 15, 2000, numerous political parties were represented: thirty-four deputies from the Liberal Democracy Party of Slovenia, fourteen from the Social Democratic Party of Slovenia, eleven from the United List of Social Democrats, nine from the Slovene People's Party, eight from the New Slovenia-Christian People's Party, four from the Democratic Party of Pensioners of Slovenia, four from the Slovene National Party, four from the Party of the Slovene Youth, and one each from both the Hungarian and Italian minorities.

The Judicial System

According to Slovenia's constitution, judges are independent in carrying out their jobs, but are always bound by the law and

National Anthem

The nation's anthem is based on the seventh stanza of France Prešeren's poem, "Zdravljica," or "The Toast," set to music by composer Stanko Premrl. This poem is thought to be one of the best political poems Prešeren ever wrote. It was originally published in 1844 in the poet's collection *Poezile*, but the censors took it out of later editions. The poem is about the need for Slovenia's freedom, equality, and caring within all the world's nations. This stanza from the poem was chosen to be the country's official anthem in 1989.

Anthem:

Zivé naj vsi naródi,
ki hrepené do"cakat' dan,
da, koder sonce hodi,
prepir iz svéta bo pregnan;
da rojak
prost bo vsak,
ne vrag, le sosed bo mejak!

English Translation:

God's blessings on all nations,
Who long and work for that bright day,
When o'er earth's habitation
No war, no strife shall hold its sway;
Who long to see
That all men free
No more shall foes, but neighbors be!

the constitution. The highest judicial body for protecting the mandates of the constitution is the Constitutional Court. It works to make sure the stipulations of the constitution are upheld, as well as protecting human rights and fundamental freedoms. It is made up of nine judges who are legal experts. They are nominated by the president and elected by the National Assembly, and each one serves for nine years.

Slovenia's judicial system also includes forty-four district courts, eleven regional courts, four higher courts, and the Supreme Court. These courts are responsible for judging those accused of crimes. Local government takes the form of 192 municipalities, which have councils and mayors that are directly elected by the people.

Ljubljana: Did You Know This?

The largest and busiest city within Slovenia is the capital, Ljubljana. Slovenian legend has it that the ancient Greek hero Jason and his companions, the Argonauts, founded the city. After they had stolen the Golden Fleece and were running from King Aites, they supposedly sailed up the Danube, into the Sava River, and into Ljubljana. There they encountered a terrible monster, which Jason bravely fought and killed. A dragon can still be found on the city's coat of arms.

Ljubljana has a long and impressive history, first mentioned in print in 1144 as the town of Laibach. During the first to sixth centuries A.D., it was referred to as the Roman town of Emona. The Habsburgs changed the name once more in the fourteenth century to Ljubljana, or "beloved." They named it in honor of the many pale-colored churches and mansions they saw there. Earthquakes almost destroyed the entire city in 1511. Between 1809 and 1814, while France had control of the area, it was the capital of the Illyrian provinces. Another quake hit in 1895, once again leveling the city.

Today, Ljubljana is a bustling city that has been compared to Paris and Prague—but more casual and calm. Its central position within Slovenia gives it a warm, temperate climate and visitors come to vacation there often. With forty-one schools, fifteen museums, thirty-five art galleries, and ten theaters, there is a great deal of culture in the area. The local university houses over 35,000 students in the city. With the Golovec Hills to the south and the Polhou Gradec Hills to the west, most of the city is laid out to the north and east. There

Tivoli Park

Živalski vrt Zoo

Tivoli Castle

TABOR

National Gallery

Ljubljanica R.

ROZNA DOLINA

Farmer's Market

Town Hall

University of Ljubljana

Ljubljana Castle

0   1200 feet

0   300 meters

VIČ

National and University Library

Slovenian Academy of Arts and Sciences

KRAKOVO

Ljubljana

are palaces to explore and a huge market (pictured below) to wander through with everything from home-made cheese to the Slovenian specialty, honey. For the more nature minded, the city is ringed with a walking path left over from the days of World War II that is perfect for an afternoon stroll. The city also boasts a beautiful zoological garden.

The buildings of the most recognized Slovenian architect, Joze Plecnik, can be seen here, as can Ljubljana Castle up on Castle Hill. Dating back to the sixteenth century, this castle is primarily used for concerts, weddings, and other public gatherings. The people of Slovenia take great pride in their capital city and people from all over the world come to visit and admire Ljubljana.

Economic Stability and Strength

A lumberyard stacked with timber for export.

SLOVENIA IS ONE OF THE MOST SUCCESSFUL COUNTRIES IN the world at making the transition from socialism to a market economy. Unlike some other new countries that have had to struggle to change, Slovenia has experienced few problems and enjoyed relative stability.

Even when Slovenia was part of Yugoslavia, it had a relatively strong economy compared with other socialist countries in Europe. It was the wealthiest of the Yugoslavian republics. Although the Slovenes only represented about 8 percent of the population at that time, they managed to produce up to 20 percent of Yugoslavia's products and exported a quarter of its goods. A common saying of that day was, "The laws are written in Belgrade, read in Zagreb, and carried out in Slovenia."

The economy faltered slightly in the 1980s as the battle for separation began to swell and, when Slovenia achieved its independence, a third of the export companies stayed with

Opposite: **Traders gather on the floor of the Ljubljana Stock Exchange.**

Economic Stability and Strength **67**

Yugoslavia. However, it didn't take long for the country to gain strength once again since it focused strongly on attracting Western European countries. Today, almost three-quarters of its trade is done with these countries, especially Germany, Italy, France, and Austria.

In the decade since Slovenia became its own country, it has focused on stabilizing the inflation that is damaging other nearby countries. The inflation rate in the Balkans soared to more than 200 percent right after independence, but now it has remained under 10 percent most of the time. Its unemployment rates run about 6.4 percent, which would be considered slightly high in the United States (with an average around 5 percent) but is quite typical in this part of the world.

Though Slovenia's unemployment rate is at 6.4 percent, these employees contribute to the economy at an auto factory.

Money Facts

As soon as the last Yugoslav soldier left Slovenia, the country issued coupons to replace the Yugoslavian dinars that had been previously used. Just about one year later, in October 1991, the Slovene tolar (SIT) was introduced. There are nine banknotes within the system, including the denominations of 10,000, 5,000, 1,000, 500, 200, 100, 50, 20, and 10 tolars.

Miljenko Licul was given the job of creating the designs for the different bills. He is the same designer that was chosen to create the 1996 Slovenian stamp commemorating the country's fifth anniversary. The Bank of Slovenia and Slovene Academy of Sciences and Arts had already chosen the people they felt represented the country's heritage and history. Licul chose to create the images in an unusual pattern of a triangle, uniting the drawing of the person with the tool he used in his field and the product it resulted in.

Portraits on the different bills are the work of artist Rudi Spanzel and they feature a frontal view as well as a silhouette of the person's head and shoulders. The tolars are dedicated as follows:

10,000 tolars	Author Ivan Cankar (1876–1918)
5,000 tolars	Painter Ivana Kobilca (1861–1926)
1,000 tolars	Poet France Prešeren (1800–1849)
500 tolars	Architect Joze Plecnik (1800–1848)
200 tolars	Composer Iacobus Gallus (1550–1591)
100 tolars	Painter Rihard Jakopic (1869–1943)
50 tolars	Mathematician Jurij Vega (1754–1802)
20 tolars	Chronicler Janez Vajkard Valvasor (1641–1693)
10 tolars	Reformer Primož Trubar (1508–1586)

All the bills are created with wonderful colors and are quite cheerful looking. The first one was put into circulation in September 1992 and the last one, the 5,000 tolar, was put into circulation in July 2002.

Originally the tolar was divided up into 100 stotinov but these aluminum coins are almost obsolete now. They have been replaced with brass coins. Unlike the bills, the Slovenian coins feature different images taken from nature. In denominations of 1, 2, 5, and 10 tolars, the coins feature images of an ibex, swallow, grasshopper, or trout, and the unique *Proteus anguinus*.

Weights and Measurements

Slovenia uses the metric system.

Imports and Exports

Unlike some other countries, that have a wide—and often negative—balance between how much they import and how much they export, Slovenia's numbers are quite close. Their annual exports are U.S.$9.3 billion and consist primarily of manufactured goods, machinery and equipment, and chemicals to Germany, Italy, Croatia, France, and Austria. Their annual imports are U.S.$10.1 billion, primarily machinery and equipment, manufactured goods, and chemicals from the same countries.

A lot of changes have occurred in the agricultural region of Slovenia. In the 1960s, half the people here made their living through some form of farming. Today, that figure is only

A very small number of Slovenes make their living by farming. The average farm is only about 8 acres (3 ha).

about one in ten. Farms are small, averaging about only 8 acres (3 ha) each. About a third of those farms produce wine. Cattle breeding is popular in Slovenia, thanks to all of its grasslands. Other agricultural products from the area include wheat, corn, pork, milk, potatoes, and orchard fruits such as apples, cherries, pears, and plums.

Manufacturing and mining are continually growing in this country. Jesenice is known for its steelworks

A lower Alpine meadow serves well for cattle.

plants, Kranj for its textile mills, and Trbovlje and Hrastnik for their coal mines. About 46 percent of the people are employed in manufacturing, and another 46 percent in service industries.

There are currently over 144,000 registered companies throughout Slovenia, and most are involved with some aspect

Almost half of Slovenia's employed work in manufacturing. Here, foundry workers pour molten metal into molds.

What Slovenia Grows, Makes, and Mines

Agriculture

Wheat	195,000 tons
Apples	22,000 tons
Milk	380 million liters

Manufacturing (in SIT)

Chemicals	46,063
Textiles	19,800
Machinery	17,189

Mining

Natural Stone	350,000 tons
Lime	150,000 tons
Aluminum	100,000 tons

of trade and commerce. Others businesses are services, real estate, construction, transport, and communications. More than 90 percent of the companies have been classified as small business enterprises.

Another step that Slovenia is taking to help ensure a strong economy for now and the future is to focus on expanding the number of foreign investments in their country. In an attempt to attract more European companies to locate in their country, Slovenia emphasizes its closeness to the sea for transportation, a dependable and skilled labor force, a stable and democratic government, and rapid economic growth. Apparently, the plan is working and more European businesses are coming to Slovenia to set up factories, offices, and warehouses.

French Renault cars are assembled at a plant in Novo Mesto, and kitchen appliances are manufactured for several German and British companies.

Tourism

A growing area of income for Slovenia is the more than 1 million tourists who come to the country each year. Most come to vacation from neighboring states like Germany, Italy, Austria, and Croatia, but they also arrive from places farther

Tourists in Slovenia amount to more than 1 million. Here, visitors tour Bled Castle.

The Business of Health at Rogaška Slatina

Slovenia is full of thermal mineral springs, mostly found in the eastern Pannonian region. Over seventy-eight sources have already been identified, three-fourths of which were discovered quite by accident. When people drilled wells in hopes of finding petroleum, they found mineral waters instead. Although rather disappointed at first, they soon changed their minds as they saw the potential profit of these unique waters.

Feeling depressed or tired? Stressed out or having some indigestion? Need to lose some weight? If so, these mineral waters might just be just what you need. Many people look for relaxation and rejuvenation in one of Slovenia's nineteen health spas. One favorite can be found at Rogaška Slatina, Slovenia's oldest and largest spa town. Located almost 80 miles (130 km) northeast of Ljubljana, this city's hotel (pictured) is known for its therapeutic spas and healthful mineral waters.

Slovenian legend has it that the spring at Rogaška Slatina was first discovered by the Greek winged horse Pegasus when he advised the god Apollo to drink from it. The spring wasn't officially put on the map until 1574, however, when Peter Zrinjski, a Croat feudal lord, drank some of the water upon the advice of his doctor. He felt so much better that he told everyone about it and word spread rapidly. Simple peasants to members of royalty came pouring into the area. For 100 years, people came to the spa in search of the healing water and by the turn of the eighteenth century, over 20,000 bottles were being sold every year. In 1803 the hotel was converted to a health resort and in only thirty years, business was so good that more hotels had to be built to keep up with the demand.

In the 1990s, war almost destroyed the health resort town. However, in recent years it has returned to full capacity. Although Slovenia has nineteen natural health and spa resorts scattered throughout the country, Rogaška Slatina remains the most popular. Today the water from this resort is still being bottled and shipped all over the world. The hotels feature a huge variety of health treatments from the simple—massage, mineral baths, and saunas—to the complex—plastic and cosmetic surgery. This is the city people often go to for vacationing, too. The town has tennis courts, archery fields, fitness centers, whirlpools, and everything else a tourist could want to relax and recover.

The Soča River is the setting for canoeing classes and kayaking competitions.

away, such as Great Britain and the Netherlands. Even the amount of people coming from the United States is growing. Many Americans are attracted to the winter sports offered in Slovenia, including skiing, snowboarding, mountain climbing, and hiking. Others come for cycling and mountain biking or caving. It's a rare country that allows a person to spend the morning rushing down a mountain of snow, and the afternoon catching rays out on the beach.

The different waterways in Slovenia offer everything from kayaking, canoeing, and rafting to other sports such as fishing, sailing, and windsurfing. Other visitors come for the opportunities in the sky: paragliding is quite popular, hot air balloon rides are offered, and, of course, for those who want to stay on land, there's terrific bird-watching opportunities. In 1997, tourists brought well over one billion U.S. dollars to the economy and that number continues to rise. As of fall 2003, U.S.$1 was equal to about 216 Slovenian tolars. A cup of coffee in Slovenia would cost about 85 cents, gas is 75 cents per liter, and a snack on the street about 90 cents. A mid-range hotel room runs about U.S.$55 a night, and dinner out for two about U.S.$40.

Proud
Slovenes

THE PEOPLE OF SLOVENIA ARE PROUD OF THEIR COUNTRY and worked hard to see that it obtained its independence. Most of the people in Slovenia are Slovenes, but there are also a number of Croats and Serbs who live throughout the country and many more cross the border daily to work. Surprisingly, the official minorities in the country are the Italians and Hungarians, which are present in somewhat smaller numbers than Croats and Serbs. The Italian and Hungarian minorities each have a representative or deputy in parliament whose job it is to monitor and maintain their rights under the constitution. They have a guaranteed right to education in their native languages, their languages must be used in local government issues, and personal documents are also in dual languages.

In recent years, migrants from other countries have headed to Slovenia in high numbers. In 2000, an overwhelming 35,000 illegal immigrants crossed into the country in hopes of finding a better life, but were arrested by the police. The vast majority came from Croatia, Iran, Romania, and Turkey. In fact, since 1995, the number

Opposite: **Slovenes, a Slavic ethnic group, make up 87 percent of the population.**

A Bosnian woman and her son eat in a refugee camp in Slovenia.

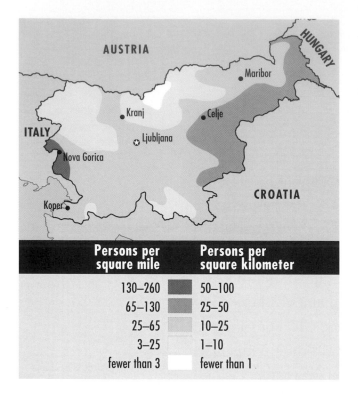

Persons per square mile	Persons per square kilometer
130–260	50–100
65–130	25–50
25–65	10–25
3–25	1–10
fewer than 3	fewer than 1

Population of Major Cities

Ljubljana	281,913
Maribor	135,863
Kranj	52,360
Novo Mesto	51,717
Celje	50,239
Koper	47,983
Nova Gorica	43,249
Velenje	34,742

of illegal immigrants caught coming from Croatia has gone up 543 percent. Yet the police suspect that they only get about one in three who are crossing the border.

Slovene Minorities

In Slovenia certain very small minorities are governed by the country's legislation: Hungarian, Italians (and to a lesser extent Roma, or Gypsy). The two largest minorities within Slovenia are actually the Serbs (from Serbia) and Croats (from Croatia). Why are the largest groups ignored in the government while the smaller ones are allowed representation and protected by laws? That is a question that is asked often—and so far, not answered— in some political circles. It is especially puzzling as the Serbs have lived in the area as far back as 1530 and the region was originally called the Kingdom of the Serbs, Croats, and Slovenes.

For one thing, the Croats and Serbs within Slovenia do not stand out as minorities. While their language is different from Slovene, it is similar enough to communicate easily. Their appearance, from eyes and hair to skin, is just like the Slovenes and they do not live in one specific area of the country. Nonetheless, many Serbs and Croats consider themselves as distinct or separate from the Slovenes.

At the same time that people from other nations are pouring into Slovenia, the country also has one of the highest rates of emigration in Europe. Some Slovenes leave for economic reasons, while others do so for political ones. About 400,000 Slovenes live outside the country. Three-quarters of these are in the United States and Canada. Approximately 50,000 live in Italy, 15,000 in Austria, and 5,000 in Hungary.

Between the years of 1880 and 1920, an amazing 330,000 Slovenes migrated to Cleveland, Ohio, in search of work. So many Slovenes came to this Ohio city that, at that time, it ranked second in the world for Slovenian population—only the country's capital of Ljubljana was bigger. Slovenian families established many small business in Cleveland from grocery stores and bakeries to furniture stores and taverns. Today, according to the last survey numbers, about 124,437 Slovenes live in the United States, with about 50,000 of these in Cleveland, Ohio. The city now features nine Slovenian centers, three church centers, and two schools that offer instruction in the Slovene language.

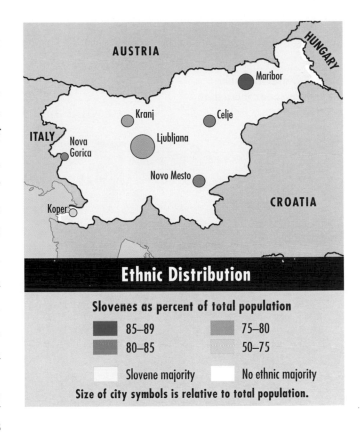

Ethnic Distribution

Slovenes as percent of total population

■	85–89	■	75–80
■	80–85	■	50–75
□	Slovene majority	□	No ethnic majority

Size of city symbols is relative to total population.

Who Lives in Slovenia?

Slovenes	87.84%
Croats	2.76%
Serbs	2.44%
Bosnians	1.36%
Hungarians	0.43%
Montenegrins	0.22%
Macedonians	0.22%
Albanians	0.18%
Italians	0.16%

A Look at the Language

Almost everyone in Slovenia speaks more than one language. Over three-quarters of them are fluent in Croatian and Serbian, while half know German and a third know English.

Most Slovenes are multilingual, or speak more than one language.

The language spoken in Slovenia is called Slovenian and is an Indo-European language. Today, it is considered to be in the South Slavic branch of languages, along with Croatian, Serbian, Macedonian, and Bulgarian. Virtually all 2 million people of the country speak Slovenian, but with a great number of dialects depending on what region they live in. Researchers aren't sure how many different dialects there are, but agree that there are at least seven or eight major ones, with as many as forty-six individual ones. Dialects are divided into seven regional groups: Carinthian, Upper Carniolan, Lower Carniolan, Littoral, Rovte, Styrian, and Pannonian.

The Slovenian language has three ways of using nouns, pronouns, verbs, and adjectives. There are singulars and plurals as in English, but with a third form for dual, or two. In other words, they have different forms of a word if one person,

Common Phrases

Dober dan	Hello
Na svidenje	Goodbye
Kako ste?	How are you?
Koliko stane?	How much is it?
Koliko je ura?	What time is it?
Samo trenutek.	Just a minute.
Oprostite.	I'm sorry.
Ne razumem.	I don't understand.

A Look at Slovenian Proverbs

One way to get a feeling for what a society is like is to look at some of the most common proverbs or sayings they use. Here are several of the ones Slovenes like:

It is easier to believe than to go and ask.

Every road does not lead to Rome.

Speak the truth, but leave immediately after.

Never whisper to the deaf or wink at the blind.

Nettles are never frostbitten.

Only lend a friend what you cannot afford to lose.

Advertising posters display the characters used in Slovenian spelling.

two people, or more than two people are involved. The Slovenes keep this archaic, or very old, form of the language as part of their national identity—it makes them more unusual and unique.

Slovenian ABC's

The Slovene alphabet is Latin and it has only twenty-five characters.

a b c č d e f g h i j k l m n o p r s š t u v z ž

The C, S and Z have carons or a ˇ to indicate they are different letters.

The C with a caron is pronounced like the "ch" in chilly.

The S with a caron is pronounced like the "sh" in should.

The Z with a caron in pronounced like "zh" like in "su" in measure.

The Slovene j is pronounced like the "y" in yes.

Lj is pronounced like the "li" in million.

Nj is pronounced like the "ni" in opinion.

R is rolled like in Spanish or Scottish.

As in English, some vowels and consonants change the sound they make depending on where they are in the word.

L is pronounced as 'w' if it's at the end of a syllable or before a vowel; the rest of the time it is pronounced like the English version.

V is pronounced as 'w' if it's at the end of a syllable or before a vowel; the rest of the time it is pronounced like the English version.

Many of the Slovene words have no vowels in them at all (vrt=garden) and some have consonant clusters like kljuc (key). The vowels in Slovenian are the same as in English: a, e, i, o, u. Like their English counterparts, they change sounds depending on the word.

Faith and Tradition

Early Christian artwork is displayed in the Dance of Death frescoes in the Hrastovlje church.

T HE HISTORY OF SLOVENIA SHOWS A NUMBER OF CHANGES in religion. Archaeological discoveries have indicated the presence of Christianity in the region dating all the way back to the late second century A.D. In the sixth and seventh centuries, a variety of missionaries began attempting to convert the Slavs, and finally, in 745, a Carantanian prince named Borut accepted Christianity. In time, most of the country of what was then called Carantania followed Borut and converted to Christianity.

Major Religions

Religion	Percentage
Roman Catholic	68.8%
Uniate Catholic	2%
Lutheran	1%
Muslim	1%
Other	22.9%

Opposite: **Christianity has been a mainstay in Slovenia since the second century A.D.**

In 1461 the diocese, or religious region, was established in Ljubljana. In the fifteenth century, all Jews were banished from the area when the Ottomans took over. By the middle of the sixteenth century, Lutheranism and Protestantism spread across the land. This was suppressed by the Roman Catholic Church at the beginning of the seventeenth century, and today Catholicism is the main religion of the country. There is an archbishop in Ljubljana and bishops are in place at both Maribor and Koper.

Archbishop Franc Rodé

Born in 1934 in the capital city of Ljubljana, Franc Rodé was appointed archbishop of the city in 1997 by Pope John Paul II. As a child, he lived in both Lienz, Austria, and Buenos Aires, Argentina. In 1960, he was ordained a Catholic priest and obtained a doctorate in theology from the Catholic Institute of Paris. Five years later, he returned to Slovenia and worked as a teacher of various theology college courses. He wrote a number of articles for various Slovenian publications and has authored several books.

In 1981 Rodé went to the Vatican and held the post of Secretary of Papal Council for Culture. He did quite a bit of traveling throughout Slovenia and other countries for public speaking engagements, and French president Jacques Chirac nominated him Knight for Merit. On March 5, 1997, Rode was appointed archbishop, succeeding Dr. Alojzij Šuštar.

A Daunting Task

Over 400 years ago, in the late sixteenth century, a Protestant writer and theologian named Jurij Dalmatin (1547–1589) took on an overwhelming task. He sat down to translate the Old and New Testaments of the Bible into the Slovene language. This was no small job since Dalmatin had no dictionaries, grammar books, or any kind of formal education to help or guide him. In fact, it took him ten years to finally complete the work.

His incredible translation was printed in Wittenberg, Germany, in 1584 and shipped back to Slovenia hidden in boxes and barrels because the Catholic Church would not have approved of having the Bible translated from Latin into the native language. This translation is one of the first Bible translations in the entire world and it helped to develop both the Slovenian culture and its perspective on religion.

The Role of Religion

Religion doesn't appear to play a large part in the modern Slovene's life. There is separation of church and state and religious education is not allowed to be part of any school's curriculum. Churches are rarely even half full on the average Sunday morning. Only religious holidays such as Easter,

Easter mass being celebrated

Christmas, and the Assumption of Mary fill up all of the seats. Easter is a major holiday. Bells are not used on most churches between Good Friday and Easter Sunday. On Palm Sunday, Slovenes commonly take an olive branch to church with them so that their priest can bless it. They also fill up a wooden basket with food like eggs and cake and take it to the church to be blessed. Afterwards, it becomes part of their Easter Sunday dinner. And as in many other countries,

Baskets full of eggs and cakes await their blessing on Easter Sunday.

Slovenes paint eggs or decorate them with wax or engravings and then offer them to their family and friends as a sign of love and affection.

Easter is a time when eggs are painted and decorated. Eggs of one color are called *pirhi*.

In addition to the Catholic religion and its traditions, some other, older worship rites are still held in Slovenia. For example, in the town of Ptuj and surrounding hills and villages, spring usually means it is time for Kurentovanje, or the official celebration of the new season. Other countries like Hungary, Serbia, and Bulgaria share this tradition, but nowhere does it exist as extravagantly and with as much gusto as Slovenia.

Slovene churches are decorated treasures of gold and silver. This is the interior of Saint Nicholas Cathedral.

Country of Beautiful Churches

Some of the world's most beautiful churches can be found throughout Slovenia. Some of the most lovely are the Church of Holy Trinity at Hrastovlje, the Church of the Virgin Mary near Ptuj, and the Church of the Assumption near Ribnica.

One house of worship that continues to draw the admiration of tourists and locals is the Church of Saint John the Baptist on the north side of the Sava Bohinjka, near Maribor. A picture-perfect medieval church, it sits on a lake and is covered in intricate frescoes, or art made by painting directly onto damp plaster. The church dates back to the twelfth century, when it was built by Count Margrave Bernard Spanheim. Although it was originally built in the Romanesque style, different artistic styles like Baroque and neo-Gothic were added throughout the following centuries. In the early sixteenth century, it had to be extensively renovated after a fire. The church features

Church of Saint John
the Baptist

unusual frescoes of everything from Abel and Cain making their offerings to God to the beheading of the church's patron saint or a row of odd-looking angels. In the mid-1800s, the church was converted to a cathedral by Bishop Martin Slomšek. The south side of the outside wall includes a painting of the patron saint of travelers, Saint Christopher. A superstition from the Middle Ages convinced people that they would not die on any day that they saw Saint Christopher's image. To be on the safe side, people from that era painted his portrait everywhere—from roadsides to village stores and, of course, on many churches.

Frescoes decorate the interior walls around the alter of Saint John the Baptist church.

Another interesting religious site is the Zidovski Stolp, or Jewish Tower, and synagogue (house of worship) that was built in Maribor somewhere around the end of the fourteenth century. Since all of the Jews were expelled from the country in the late fifteenth century, it has been used for many other purposes than what it was intended for. Today, the city of Maribor is working to renovate it as an historic monument.

Following the God of Pleasure

Kurent is the main character of a wild carnival in the city of Ptuj. He is the God of Pleasure and people dress up like him in droves. They put on sheepskins with bells hanging from their belts. Then, they add furry hats covered in everything from feathers and sticks to ribbons and streamers. Eyeholes are cut into leather masks and big noses are common. Each mouth

The carnival spirit Kurent is believed to bring luck and an abundance of crops.

has a very long, red tongue sticking out of it.

Going door to door throughout the city, the revelers swing their wooden clubs covered in hedgehog spines and scare away any evil spirits. Young girls offer new, white handkerchiefs to Kurent and housewives may run up and smash clay pots at his feet to ensure a year of health, luck, and happiness.

Religious Calendar

Easter Sunday and Monday	March or April
Assumption of Mary Day	August 15
Reformation Day	October 31
All Souls' Day	November 1
Christmas	December 25

An 1889 illustration shows Saint Nicholas and an angel blessing a Slovenian family on Christmas.

Christmas is another big celebration in Slovenia, although it is more a celebration than a religious holiday. Previously banned, Christmas is now openly celebrated with Christmas trees and some families have Nativity scenes. Families gather together and go to Midnight Mass at their church. When they return, they open their gifts, some of which are from Bozicek (Santa Claus).

Visits from the Pope

In May 1996, Pope John Paul II visited Slovenia for the first time. He came at the invitation of then President Milan Kučan. His visit coincided with his seventy-sixth birthday, as well as the 1,250 anniversary of Christianity in the Slovene territory and the 1,000 anniversary of the Freising Manuscripts. After he returned from this visit, the pope told listeners at the Vatican that Slovenia's unique geographical location gave them the special opportunity to serve as Christian witnesses to the world.

Three years later, in September 1999, Pope John Paul II returned for a second visit (right). He was there for the beatification of Anton Martin Slomšek, a nineteenth-century bishop of Maribor. This meant that the pope declared Slomšek to be a blessed and holy person that should be revered and honored. Slomšek was known in history for promoting the idea of literacy to the Slovenes, using their native language. He is the first Slovenian to ever be so honored.

The pope addressed the people of Slovenia and blessed them with these words: "May the Blessed Virgin Mary watch over you and all your thoughts, Mother Mary the Queen of Slovenia, whom your people honor with the name Marija Pmoagaj [Mary Help Us]. I assure you, beloved Church that abides in Slovenia, I assure every branch and part of you, as well as all the Slovene people, my prayer, and from my heart I bless each and every one of you." Following the ceremony, the pope met with President Kučan and then returned to Rome.

The Arts and Sports

S LOVENIA IS A COUNTRY THAT FOCUSES HEAVILY ON MUSIC, art, and sports. Recent years have seen an amazing growth in cultural areas. For the Slovenes, as with many other countries, it is their language and their culture that has helped identify them as a nation. The state considers itself financially responsible for supporting culture and it pays for professional institutes in the fields of music, theater, preserving cultural

Opposite: **Young Slovenes take part in extreme sports.**

Slovenes like to sing and enjoy themselves.

France Prešeren

Of all the talented writers to come from Slovenia, perhaps the most loved of all is the poet France Prešeren. His statue can be found in Kranj, his words in the national anthem, and his face on the 1,000 tolar banknote. His writings helped to prove that even though the Slovene language was relatively new, it was equal to the other European languages.

Born in 1800 in the town of Vrba, Prešeren wrote his first poem at twenty-five. He wrote on and off during the following years as he worked to obtain his law degree. In 1827, one of his poems was published in a local newspaper and the following year, he graduated.

A variety of Prešeren's poems were published in poetry anthologies from 1830 to 1834. During this time, the poet was falling in and out of love. His first love was a young woman who loved another; his second, a very young girl with whom he later fathered three children; and his third, yet another woman who didn't return his feelings. All of these loves, along with a passionate desire to help see his country achieve independence, kept him inspired to write poems, including this one, entitled "The Master Theme."

A Slovene wreath your poet has entwined;
A record of my pain and of your praise,
Slice from my heart's deep roots have sprung these lays,
These tear-stained flowers of a poet's mind.

They come from where no man can sunshine find,
Unblest by soothing winds of warmer days;
Above them savage peaks the mountains raise,
Where tempests roar and nature is unkind.

They were all fed on many a plaint and tear;
Frail growth these blossoms had, so sad and few,
As over them Malignant storm-clouds flew.

Behold how weak and faded they appear!
Send but your rays their glory to renew—
Fresh flowers will spread fragrance far and near.

Between the years of 1832 and 1846, Prešeren applied for his own private legal practice five times—and was rejected each time. Finally, in 1846, he was granted a practice in Kranj and he moved. That same year, his first book of poems was published. Unfortunately, just three years later, Prešeren died from a condition called cirrhosis of the liver. Following his death, people began to pay more attention to his poetry and today, Prešeren is honored as one of Slovenia's most important persons.

heritage, maintaining the national library system of sixty branches, and publishing over 4,000 new book titles a year.

Reading and Writing

Just about twenty years ago, Slovenia was the record holder in Europe for the number of new books published per capita. Slovenes attend their libraries, checking out an average of 17 million books per year. They take great pride in their authors and honor their work. In addition to France Prešeren, some of their most treasured writers include Primož Trubar, Drago Jančar, Ivan Cankar, and Tomas Salamun.

Going to the Theater

Slovenia has ten professional theaters; two are puppet theaters and two are for opera and ballet performances. More than 650,000 people attend each year. One of the most important historical figures in the theatrical world is playwright and poet Anton Tomaz Linhart (1765–1795). In December 1789, one of his comedies was performed in the Slovene language for the first time. That date is known in Slovenia as the birthday

The opera house in Ljubljana offers operas and ballets.

The Magic of Mladinsko Theater

Almost half a century ago, the Mladinsko Theatre was opened in the capital city. Originally established to be the first professional theater for children and youth in the country, it featured traditional fairy tales and stories for two decades. In 1975, however, things changed, and the theater began looking into performances for both adults and children, focusing on the unusual and imaginative, for any age. They offered plays by Slovenian authors as well as works by T. S. Eliot, Lewis Carroll, and William Shakespeare.

Today, the theater has an international reputation for offering over 200 performances a year that are both trendy and uncommon. Their productions are so popular that they have begun touring, going to other theaters throughout Europe. The theater has also become a place for foreign festivals, classes for master performers and students, and a meeting place for various world artists.

of Slovene theater. Almost a century later, in 1867, the first Dramatics Society was founded in the capital city.

Slovenia is also rich in visual art. They have 200 galleries and more than 800 rotating temporary exhibits. The Modern

With more than 150 art galleries and temporary exhibits on display, Slovenia's art lovers have many collections to view.

The National Gallery is
Slovenia's main art museum.

Gallery in Ljubljana has more than 7,000 works of mostly
modern art, while the National Gallery displays works of the
earlier European painters and artists.

The Fight to Compete at Planica

In the early 1930s, skiing as a sport was already popular in Slovenia, thanks to all of its mountains. It was especially big in Planica, a northern part of the Julian Alps in the northwest part of the country. The more adventurous skiers attempted jumps on the mountains, but the actual sports competition of ski jumping was just getting off the ground. Ski jumps were being built in other European nations, with skiers hurtling more than 230 feet (70 m) in the air at a time. It was as close to flying as humans had ever gotten and it wasn't long before Slovenia wanted an official ski jump of its own.

In February 1934, they got one. It began with Joso Gorec, the general secretary of Yugoslavia. He worked to spread word about the goal of creating a ski jump at Planica, while engineer Stanko Bloudek and architect Ivan Rozman worked to turn it into a reality. When the ski jump opened, the men predicted that soon skiers would be breaking records and hitting jumps of more than 300 feet (90 m). This is when the International Ski Federation (FIS) became involved.

The FIS thought that ski jumps of more than 230 feet were not safe and should not be allowed in any competitions. While the issue was being discussed, Austrian skier Sepp Dradl created a new world record when he jumped 328 feet (100 m). Through a lot of diplomacy and dedication, Gorec finally convinced the FIS congress at Helsinki that the ski jump at Planica was completely safe, and they agreed. This put the Planica jump on all of the skiing competition calendars and soon people were coming from all over to try it out.

During World War II, the ski jump was temporarily forgotten and then it was damaged. As soon as the war ended, however, it was repaired and soon after, it was the site of the World Cup Competition.

Today, Planica is considered to be one of the best ski jumps in the world. In 1997 Slovenian Goran Janus jumped a record-breaking 674 feet (206 m)—literally flying through the air. In years to come, Planica will likely see more competitions and more unbelievable and breathtaking flights.

Petra Majdic of Slovenia (in the lead) competes in the women's cross country relay during the Winter Olympics in 2002.

The Popular World of Sports

Almost half of the Slovenes are actively involved in some kind of sport. The state feels that sports are in the public interest and through their National Sports Programme, the state financially supports all sports in all areas of the country. As a nation, the Slovenes compete quite well internationally. To date, they have won more than 50 Olympic medals and 360 World Championship medals in everything from skiing and rowing, to volleyball and basketball. Tourists often come to this area of the world to be a part of the skiing, mountain climbing, paragliding, boating, and hiking that is part of everyday life here.

Slovenia's Mountaineers

Two of the very first mountaineers to come out of Slovenia were Baltazar Hacquet and Valentin Stanic. Both of these men climbed the peaks of their home country in addition to many other mountains in the late eighteenth and early nineteenth centuries. They would most likely be amazed to see what kind of climbing is done in the new millennium.

Slovenes hold many of the mountain-climbing titles of the world. Slovenia's primary mountaineer today is Tomaz Humar (right). A man in his early thirties, he has made over 1,200 climbs in his lifetime, including many in Slovenia. He is known for taking on the biggest and most difficult climbs, and in one tragic trip, his partner Janez Jeglic was killed during the ascent.

One of Humar's biggest accomplishments was in 1999 when he spent an amazing nine days climbing the south wall of the Daulagiri Mountain in the Himalayas. This 26,794-foot (8,172-m) mountain has been considered one of the last great challenges in mountain climbing. He reached areas that had never been reached before and forged completely new routes. He was forced by weather and increasing risk of frostbite to stop about 328 feet (100 m) from the summit, but this was still considered to be a new record in the world of mountaineering.

Davo Karnicar and Mount Everest

The highest point in the entire world is found at Mount Everest in Nepal. At 29,035 feet (8,855 m) high, it is a continual challenge for all mountain skiers and climbers. In 2000, 38-year-old Slovenian Davo Karnicar took on that challenge. He had tried once before in 1996 but was stopped by a vicious snowstorm. He lost his index finger and little finger to frostbite in the attempt.

In 2000, along with journalists, telephone operators, technicians, and people to help carry gear, Karnicar ascended the mountain from the base camp at 17,500 feet (5,337 m) to the summit. His goal? He was hoping to be the first person ever to ski down Mount Everest without stopping.

After a less than restful night's sleep, Karnicar was ready. He strapped on his skis and began the journey—not stopping to take them off again until five hours later, when he reached base camp, an exhausting trip and altitude drop of 11,506 feet (3,509 m).

As amazing as this feat was, coming up with the finances for it was equally so. The permit to ski on Mount Everest in itself cost $70,000, let alone the cost of food, assistants, equipment, and more. To raise the money, Karnicar turned to the Internet. His descent was broadcast hour-by-hour on the World Wide Web, and pledges covered his costs.

Karnicar trained for this challenge by climbing Slovenia's Mount Triglav and Mount Blanc in the French Alps. A climber for years and former member of the Yugoslav Alpine Ski Team, he had more than 1,200 climb and ski descents under his belt. However, the descent down the southern face of Mount Everest remains one of his biggest achievements and successes.

The Slovenian soccer team poses for a group photo prior to their Euro 2000 match against Norway.

A fairly recent phenomenon in the world of Slovenian sports has been a growing interest in the game of football (the sport known as soccer in the United States). The first Slovenian Football League was put together in August 1991 and their first official international match was played in June 1992. Since then, they have gone on to play in major championships, qualifying for both the 2000 and 2002 Football World Cup.

Slovenia's Medal Winners

Slovenia has a long reputation for producing some of the world's best gymnasts. Two perfect examples are Leon Stukelj and Miroslav Cerar.

Leon Stukelj (below) has been called the most successful competitor in Slovenian history. He was born in the city of Novo Mesto in 1898. By the age of nine, he had begun to train in gymnastics. Despite his

fascination with the sport, he also went on to college and obtained a law degree, becoming a judge.

He won his first competition at Ljubljana's 1922 World Championships and continued to win medals for the next fourteen years. He won the 1926 World Championship in Lyon, the 1924 Paris Olympics, the 1928 Amsterdam Olympics, the 1936 Berlin Olympics, the 1930 World Championship in Luxembourg, the 1931 World Championship at Paris, and the 1936 Berlin Olympics. In all, he brought home a total of twenty medals: eight gold, six silver, and six bronze.

That incredible record was not broken until after World War II, when Slovenian Miroslav Cerar started his career. Born in 1937 in Ljubljana, Cerar had an incredible career from 1958 to 1970. He began competing in 1956 and two years later he won his first bronze medal at the 1958 World Championships. He followed that by winning almost every competition he was in for the next fourteen years, including the 1964 and 1968 Olympics. All in all, Cerar totaled twenty-nine bronze, silver, and gold medals. In 1999, he was inducted into the International Gymnastics Hall of Fame and since his retirement, he has served on the Slovenian Olympic Academy and the European Fair Play Movement. Recently, the Slovenian tradition in gymnastics has continued with Milos Stergar's fourth place at the 1998 World Cup competitions.

The Slovene Philharmonic Orchestra performs at the Congress and Cultural Centre in Ljubljana. The orchestra began as the Academiae Philharmonicorum Labacensis in 1701.

There are two opera houses in Slovenia, as well as five professional orchestras including the Slovene Philharmonic Orchestra. Slovene music ranges from that of the Avensiks, the founders of traditional popular music, complete with guitars, horns, and accordions, to that of Laibach, an altogether different sort of group. Few rock bands have been as challenged—or challenging—as Laibach has been for the last twenty years. Named after the German term for Ljubljana during the Habsburg reign and Nazi occupation, their name alone

The Avensiks founded a popular version of traditional Slovene music.

got them banned from playing publicly from 1983 to 1987. And that was before people heard their music.

The band began in 1980 in Trbovlje. The group was unhappy with the direction their country was going in and looking for a way to express it. They created their own band and soon after planned their first concert. The night before they were to play in 1980, they plastered their hometown with posters. By the next day, all their signs had been torn down and

Vilim Demsar

It's hard to imagine that a pail and a violin have much in common, but they do. In the late 1700s, the Demsar family was carrying on its tradition of making wooden pails out of pine. They were known for choosing just the right kind of pine to make the best pails. When Blaz Demsar was born in 1903, he soon fell into the tradition also, but he took it further. He became a skilled carpenter and soon began choosing wood to make violins instead of pails. By 1948, his instruments were being used by the masters; twelve years later his violins, violas, and violoncellos were being used by soloists around the world.

Vilim Demsar (pictured) was born in Ljubljana in 1937. He and his brother Cvetko began learning the family tradition of violin making when they were teenagers. Vilim had a natural talent for the job and began creating incredible instruments. He studied music and not only played the violin in various orchestras, but also taught it to others. In this way, he had the best understanding of how to create the perfect violin. Today, he is known the world over for the clarity and purity of his instruments and he keeps on making them from his store in the country's capital.

the concert was canceled. For others, this may have been a sign to give up, but for Laibach, it was what they needed to get going.

In 1982, they began doing concerts around Yugoslavia and that year headlined at the New Rock Festival in the capital city. A year later, they were on television. Although the name of the band kept them banned from playing locally, they took their show to other European countries and, in 1985, released their first album. Their success has been nonstop since then, despite continued controversy over their lyrics and performances.

Laibach does not perform a mellow concert. A combination of advanced electronics, smoke bombs, and projected images makes much of their music disturbing and disharmonious. This is their goal. They aren't out to entertain as much as to educate and enlighten. They point out what they believe is wrong in their country, as well as the world. In the twenty

The musical group Laibach explores the relationship between art and ideology in their music.

years since they began, they have produced fifteen records and have performed in such places as The Palace in Los Angeles and the National Theater in Sarajevo. In June 2000, people of Trbovlje who had once worked to shut them down, gave the band their annual municipal prize in recognition of their achievements both in Slovenia and in other countries. Where the band will go next is not known, but it can be certain that they won't go quietly.

Grab that Dormouse!

One tradition that has existed in Slovenia for centuries is the annual hunt for dormice. Unlike some species of rodents, dormice are edible. These gray-furred animals are about 6 inches (15 cm) long and weigh between half and a whole pound. They live in the forest and hibernate through the winter. First mentioned in the late seventeenth century by historian Valvasor and again one hundred years later by botanist and explorer Balthazar Houquet, they are considered to be the primary kind of hunting animal in the country. During the seventeenth to the nineteenth centuries, rural Slovenes in search of extra food did most of the hunting. The meat was often baked, roasted, or smoked, then served with soups or vegetables. Later, during the wars, the people from towns joined in the hunt. Dormice are still served in Slovenia today, but are considered more of a delicacy.

Dormice were usually caught in September and October before they went in to hibernation. Hunters would set out wooden traps by trees, baited with fruit or nuts. A good season might garner several thousand of the dormice, with some traps fetching up to 100 mice a night. Today's traps are made of steel or iron and are bought as Slovenian souvenirs as often as actual traps.

Originally, these dormice were used for food, as well as for their hide and fat. The grease was used for medicinal purposes and could once fetch a decent price. The animal's hides were also sold and exported to other European countries. Now neither one are sold and Slovenians only use the hides to make the traditional dormouse fur winter cap, considered to be an object of national identity.

While dormice hunting is not as popular and certainly not as necessary as it once was, the tradition does continue. There are four dormouse associations in the country and they usually meet for social reasons. The largest of the groups is responsible for maintaining the Sneznik Castle in central Slovenia. Here, tourists who want to know more about the dormouse hunting tradition can see 260 different traps and demonstrations of how hunters lived and made use of all parts of the animal.

Daily Life

AILY LIFE IN SLOVENIA IS FULL OF BOTH THE COMMON and the unusual. Families make meals, adults go off to work, and children go off to school. They speak in a language that may seem complicated to foreigners, yet the entire country is literate. The majority of the people are between 15 and 64 years old; the percentage of those under and over those ages is almost equal. The average life expectancy has improved dramatically in recent decades, reaching 70 years for men and almost 78 for women. Half of the people in Slovenia have homes in the city, or urban areas; half are in the country, or rural areas. Almost half of them work in service industries, the other half in manufacturing and only 8 percent are involved in agriculture.

Opposite: **Daily life in Slovenia is similar to that of other countries. Here, a woman purchases fresh vegetables for her evening meal.**

Slovenes live full and enriching lives with half of the population choosing an urban lifestyle and the remaining half, rural.

National Holidays

New Year's	January 1 and 2
Prešeren Day	February 8
Easter Sunday and Monday	March or April
Day of Uprising Against Occupation	April 27
Labor Day	May 1 and 2
National Day	June 25
Assumption Day	August 15
Reformation Day	October 31
All Souls' Day	November 1
Christmas	December 25
Independence Day	December 26

On the Menu

The people of Slovenia eat a rich and rather varied diet. Many of the dishes they have as parts of their regular fare tend to be borrowed from the lands around them. From their Austrian neighbors, they have incorporated *klobasa*, or sausage, and *zavitek*, or strudel. From Italy comes *njoki* (potato dumplings) and from Hungary comes *golaz* (goulash) and *paprikas* (chicken or beef stew). Much of their food is based on meat, including venison, fish, veal, and pork. Mushrooms, which grow all over the country's woods, are usually part of the meal somewhere—from a sauce to a stew. Wine, of course, is a common accompaniment also, since it is produced in large quantities. Honey has been the sweetener of choice for these people for a long time.

A Sweet Tradition

Beekeeping is a tradition in Slovenia. Sixth-century Slovenes brought beehives with them in oval logs. Anton Jansa (1734–1773), a Slovene, was the first official teacher of beekeeping at the court of Empress Maria Theresa of Vienna. He wrote two books on the topic. In 1781, the first beekeeping association was established and it continues today under the name Beekeepers' Association of Slovenia.

There are over 9,500 beekeepers in the country, with a total of more than 165,000 beehives. The hives are kept in wooden bee houses called *ulnjaki*. Many beekeepers paint the

Unique painted beehives of Slovenia.

Beekeepers process the honey from their hives and export more than 300 tons to neighboring countries.

fronts of these beehives, creating a new art form. Over 300 tons of honey are exported to countries like Germany and Austria each year, and although the number of beekeepers has decreased in recent years, it will continue to be part of the country's heritage. The Carnolian race of honeybee is famous for its gentle disposition and productive habits.

Of Dandelions and *Buhteljni*

Visitors who come to Slovenia in the spring have noticed the natives doing something odd. They walk through the fields and meadows very slowly, apparently looking for something. Every so often, they bend over, cut something off, put it into a bag, and then return to searching. They are looking for tender, young dandelion shoots. When they have enough, they take them home and use them in a number of different spring dishes, such as this one:

$10\frac{1}{2}$ ounce dandelion shoots, washed and dried

2 medium potatoes, cooked, peeled, and sliced

1 hard-boiled egg, sliced

1 clove garlic, finely chopped

2 tablespoons of lard

vinegar to taste

salt to taste

Put hot potatoes on dandelion shoots to soften them; add egg and sprinkle with garlic. Heat lard in saucepan and allow cracklings to fry for 30 seconds. Add vinegar and salt, then mix and pour over the dandelion shoots. Toss to serve.

Note: Be sure not to pick dandelions from an area that has been sprayed with weed killers and pesticides.

Another favorite dish, especially among Slovenian children is *Buhteljni*, a sweet dessert.

1 pound white flour

$1\frac{1}{4}$ ounces fresh yeast

3 ounces butter

$\frac{4}{5}$ cup warm milk

1 tablespoon honey

2 eggs

pinch of salt

apricot jam or orange marmalade

melted butter

powdered sugar

Sift the flour into a bowl and make a small hollow in the center. Crumble the yeast into a cup and then add 1 teaspoon sugar, 2 tablespoons flour, and cup warm milk. Mix it all together well and then pour the yeast mixture into the hollow in the flour and set it in a warm place to rise. When it has doubled in size, mix the flour with the yeast, 3 ounces of butter, sugar, eggs, and salt and knead well to form a smooth dough. Set it in a warm place to rise again.

Dust a flat surface with flour and roll out the dough to "half the thickness of your finger," or about 3/10 (8 mm) of an inch. Cut the dough into 3 x 3 inch (8 x 8 cm) squares. Put 1 teaspoon of jam on each one and then fold the corners above the jam, squeezing lightly to make the dough stick together. Dip each one in melted butter and set in a medium-high baking dish, making sure that the edges of the pastries are touching. Set the baking dish in a warm place to rise again about double in size.

Preheat the oven to about 350°F (180°C) and bake until well browned, about 45 minutes. Remove from the oven and allow to cool. When completely cooled off, dust with powdered sugar, divide them, and eat!

A Slovenian meal usually begins with soup and then moves into the main course. This is typically a meat dish and quite often will be turkey, goose, fish, or other seafood. Chicken isn't as popular in Slovenia as it is in some other countries. Dessert follows and in Slovenia, that can be a real

A family dines on traditional Slovenian dishes.

Potica, a Slovene specialty, is served on festive occasions.

treat. Two national favorites are potica and gibanica. *Potica* is a nut roll that is often filled with a variety of things and is served with a cup of tea or coffee. *Gibanica* is a pastry that is filled with poppy seeds, walnuts, apples, and cheese and then topped off with a generous serving of cream.

Mid-day snacks, or even a light meal, are common for Slovenes. One local favorite is the *burek*. Bought at outdoor stands in many different locations, it is a light pastry that is filled with meat and cheese and sometimes apple. It is inexpensive and filling—but, like the desserts, not low in calories.

Though many couples prefer not to wed, many others do wed, usually in their late twenties.

Getting Married, Staying Married—or Not

The number of marriages in Slovenia has dropped in half in the last two decades, while the number of couples who choose to live together outside of marriage is growing rapidly. Not only are Slovenes getting married less, they are also thinking about it longer before making the decision. In 2000 the average age of men and women at their first marriage was 29.6 for men and 26.7 for women. Waiting to get married hasn't helped the divorce rate much, however. The rate is up to over 2,000 couples per year, or 30 percent. This is still lower than the United States rate, which usually runs around 50 percent.

In addition to later marriages and increasing divorces, the Slovene people have fewer babies than many other developed countries. They average fewer than 10 births per 1,000; the world average is well over double that (22 per 1,000). Their neighbors (Italy, Croatia, Hungary) average about the same, with Croatia leading the group at 12.82 births per 1,000.

Going to School

Slovenia is considered a very well educated country and has just a little less than a 100 percent literacy rate. Knowing how to read and write is a truly elemental part of their culture. When someone asks a fellow Slovene what their last name is, they say, "Kako si pisete?" which translated means, "How do you write yourself?"

Elementary school, which previously had been for eight years, now lasts for nine in certain schools throughout Slovenia. This is a fairly new change to the system and only a

fraction of the schools are currently participating, although all will by the end of 2003. The decision was made in order to improve the overall educational levels of the people. Apparently, it is working. More young people are staying in school and more are graduating. The class of 2000 exceeded 10,000 graduates for the first time in the country's history.

Elementary schools are everywhere in Slovenia. At last count there were 814, with an admirable ratio of 12 students per teacher. Children begin at the age of six, and the nine years are divided up into three three-year segments. Virtually all students who complete elementary school go on to secondary education, which is usually separated into either vocational schools, technical schools, or *grimnazije* (grammar school). The country has 144 secondary schools. Grammar school (which is equivalent to high school in the United States) provides preparations for higher education like university or college. There are sixty-nine higher education establishments in the country.

Keeping Current and In Touch

Slovenes have many ways to stay in contact with the news and with each other. There are six major daily newspapers published in Slovenia, along with almost fifty others that are

Slovenia publishes many newspapers for its citizens. This man holds a copy at a demonstration for the country's independence.

issued weekly or in individual regions. Some of the most popular are the *Ljubljanske Novice*, *Delo*, and *Vecer*. Magazines range from entertainment tabloids to professional journals and include titles like *Nasa Zena*, *Connect*, and *Slovenia Weekly*.

Slovenia has forty-eight different television stations; three are national and the rest are through cable. However, more people prefer to listen to the radio. The country has 177 radio stations to choose from and more people have radios than televisions in this country. People here listen to the radio an average of three or more hours each day.

Over 1 million Slovenes have cell phones now, and 30 percent of the country is hooked into the Internet. Currently,

Modern technology has taken hold in Slovenia with more than 1 million owning cell phones.

there are eleven different Internet Service Providers and about 600,000 Slovenes go online each day.

Of course, a number of the people spend their time involved in sports—either playing them or watching them.

These Slovenian boys make use of computers and the Internet.

A golf course in Bled.

Some ski or snowboard; others like to climb small mountains, go paragliding or just spend the day out in a boat on one of the many bodies of water there are to choose from. A majority of Slovenes have developed into big football (or soccer) fans;

others enjoy nature through hiking and walking. For those who are in the mood for something truly original and challenging, there is a new game to enjoy.

In 1999 Kranj was the host to a sport that is gaining international popularity—the European Underwater Hockey Championships. Played on the bottom of a swimming pool, it requires teamwork, agility—and strong lungs.

Underwater hockey is for both men and women but oxygen tanks aren't allowed, so players must work together to synchronize their trips to the surface for a quick breath. A team is made up of six people with four substitutes on each side, although it can be adapted for more or less than that. A game is thirty minutes long with a three-minute break halfway through. Just as in basketball, there is no blocking, holding, or guarding allowed. The only equipment needed is a mask, fins, snorkel, protective glove, stick, and puck. The first three items can be found in most sports stores; the stick, glove, and puck usually are special ordered from companies catering to this new sport. Almost anything that is weighted and easily seen can be used as goals, although special cones can also be bought.

Although Slovenia is a rather young country, it is already establishing itself as a place with a long and rich heritage, beautiful and fertile land, and a fascinating culture. As tourists continue to discover it and the country continues to grow and strengthen, it will become easier and easier to find on any map.

Timeline

Slovenian History		World History	
		2500 B.C.	Egyptians build the Pyramids and the Sphinx in Giza.
		563 B.C.	The Buddha is born in India.
		A.D. 313	The Roman emperor Constantine recognizes Christianity.
Slavic ancestors settle in the area of present Slovenia.	A.D. 500s	610	The Prophet Muhammad begins preaching a new religion called Islam.
The first Slovene state, Slavic Duchy of Carantania, is formed.	600s		
Carantania is taken over by the Frankish Empire; Slavs convert to Christianity and lose their independence.	745		
Beginning of Slovene nation.	800s		
Freising manuscripts are written.	972–1022	1054	The Eastern (Orthodox) and Western (Roman) Churches break apart.
		1066	William the Conqueror defeats the English in the Battle of Hastings.
		1095	Pope Urban II proclaims the First Crusade.
		1215	King John seals the Magna Carta.
All the Slovene area is under rule of the Habsburgs, later known as the Austro-Hungarian Empire (except for the brief period of 1809–1814).	1300–1918	1300s	The Renaissance begins in Italy.
		1347	The Black Death sweeps through Europe.
Turkish invasion begins.	1400s	1453	Ottoman Turks capture Constantinople, conquering the Byzantine Empire.
		1492	Columbus arrives in North America.
Literacy is an accepted concept and the first printed book is printed.	1550	1500s	The Reformation leads to the birth of Protestantism.
The Bible is translated into Slovenian.	1584		

Slovenian History

Slovenia temporarily under Napoleon **1809–1814**
Bonaparte's control and known as part of
the Illyrian Provinces.

Kingdom of the Croats, Serbs, and **1918**
Slovenes is formed.

World War II ends; Federal People's **1945**
Republic of Yugoslavia is declared.

First democratic elections held; 88.5 **1990**
percent of the voters choose independence.

Slovenia declares its independence; **1991**
Yugoslav army attacks; Brioni Declaration
is signed, ending the military involvement.

European nations officially recognize **1992**
Slovenia; it becomes a member of the
United Nations.

Slovenia becomes a founding member of **1994**
the World Trade Organization.

European Union (EU) accepts Slovenia as **1996**
associate partner.

Slovenia becomes a nonpermanent member **1998**
of United Nations Security Council.

World History

1776	The Declaration of Independence is signed.
1789	The French Revolution begins.
1865	The American Civil War ends.
1914	World War I breaks out.
1917	The Bolshevik Revolution brings communism to Russia.
1929	Worldwide economic depression begins.
1939	World War II begins, following the German invasion of Poland.
1945	World War II ends.
1957	The Vietnam War starts.
1969	Humans land on the moon.
1975	The Vietnam War ends.
1979	Soviet Union invades Afghanistan.
1983	Drought and famine in Africa.
1989	The Berlin Wall is torn down, as communism crumbles in Eastern Europe.
1991	Soviet Union breaks into separate states.
1992	Bill Clinton is elected U.S. president.
2000	George W. Bush is elected U.S. president.
2001	Terrorists attack World Trade Towers, New York, and the Pentagon, Washington, D.C.

Fast Facts

Official name: Republic of Slovenia

Capital: Ljubljana

Official language: Slovenian

Ljubljana

Slovenia's flag

Soča River

Religion(s):	Roman Catholic; Uniate Catholic; Lutheran; Muslim; other
National anthem:	"The Toast" by France Prešeren
Type of government:	Parliamentary democratic republic
Chief of state:	President
Head of government:	Prime minister
Area of country:	7,825 square miles (20,273 sq km)
Latitude and longitude:	46° 07' N, 14° 49' E
Lowest elevation:	0 at sea level
Highest elevation:	Mount Triglav, 9,400 feet (2,864 m)
Average temperature extremes:	As high as 100°F (37.7°C) in the summer and below 32°F (0°C) in the northeast regions
Average precipitation:	31 inches (79 cm) in the east and 117 inches (297 cm) in northwest
National population (1991 est.):	1,965,986

Population of largest largest cities:

Ljubljana	300,000
Maribor	135,863
Kranj	52,360
Novo Mesto	51,717
Celje	50,239

Church of Saint John
the Baptist

Currency

Famous landmarks: ▶ *Vrsic Pass in Julian Alps*, Triglav National Park

▶ *Dolenjska Museum*, Novo Mesto

▶ *Saltworks Museum*, Sečovlje

▶ *Beekeeping Museum*, Radovljica

▶ *Bled Castle*, Postojna

▶ *Church of Saint John the Baptist*, Bohinj

Industry: Industry is evenly divided between manufacturing and services. Agriculture plays a much smaller part and is primarily in vineyards, fruit orchards, and cattle breeding.

Currency: Slovenes have a tolar system using bills in increments of 10 tolars to 100,000 and brass coins in denominations of 1, 2, 5, and 10 tolars.

System of weights and measures: Metric system

Literacy rate: 99.6%

Hiking trail

Janez Drnovšek

Common Slovenian phrases:

Dober dan	Hello
Na svidenje	Goodbye
Kako ste?	How are you?
Koliko stane?	How much is it?
Koliko je ura?	What time is it?
Samo trenutek.	Just a minute.
Oprostite.	I'm sorry.
Ne razumem.	I don't understand.

Famous Slovenians:

Ivan Cankar   (1876–1918)
The country's most loved short story writer

Janez Drnovšek   (1950–)
Current president

Ivana Kobilca   (1861–1926)
Important female painter

Joze Plecnik   (1872–1957)
Architect

France Prešeren   (1800–1849)
Poet and national hero

To Find Out More

Books

▶ Fallon, Steve, and Neil Wilson. *Slovenia*, 3rd edition. Victoria, Australia: Lonely Planet Publications, 2001.

▶ Hicyilmaz, Gaye. *Smiling for Strangers*. New York: Farrar, Straus and Giroux, 2000.

Web Sites

▶ **The CIA World Factbook for Slovenia**
www.cia.gov/cia/publications/factbook/geos/si.html
Extensive statistics and look at all aspects of the country.

▶ **Virtual Guide to Slovenia**
http://www.matkurja.com/eng/country-info/
Includes individual sections on arts and culture, the economy, history, and more.

▶ **Lonely Planet Guide**
http://www.lonelyplanet.com/destinations/europe/slovenia/facts.htm
A travel guide to Slovenia including history and major places to visit.

▶ **World InfoZone**
http://www.worldinfozone.com/facts.php?country=Slovenia
Thirteen separate sections about Slovenia including a list of interesting facts.

▶ **Slovenia Mission to the United Nations**
http://www.un.int/slovenia/facts.html
Six sections covering defense, foreign policy, and more.

▶ **Slovene National Tourist Board**
www.slovenia-tourism.si
Official Web site with information about the country specifically geared to visitors.

Organizations

▶ **Embassy of the Republic of Slovenia**
1525 New Hampshire Avenue NW
Washington, D.C. 20036
(202) 667-5363

▶ **Consulate of the Republic of Slovenia**
1111 Chester Ave., Suite 520
Cleveland, OH 44114
(216) 589-9220

▶ **Permanent Mission of the Republic of Slovenia to the United Nations**
600 Third Ave., 24th Floor
New York, NY 10016
(212) 370-3007

▶ **Slovene Chamber of Commerce**
Gospodarska zbornica Slovenije
Dimièeva 13
SI-1504 Ljubljana
+ 386 1 589 80 00

Index

Page numbers in *italics* indicate illustrations.

Meet the Author

TAMRA ORR is a writer and author living in Portland, Oregon. She is the homeschooling mother to four and author of more than two dozen books for children and families, including *School Violence: Halls of Hope, Halls of Fear* for Franklin Watts and Enchantment of the World *Turkey* for Children's Press. She writes regularly for a number of national educational testing companies for grades K–12. In her few rare spare minutes a day, she loves to read, talk to her family, and stare at the beautiful mountains of the northwest.

Researching this book was a pleasure for Orr. She spent time in a pool, trying to imagine playing underwater hockey, and wondering just how she would really feel about eating dormice in her vegetable soup. Downloading one of Laibach's songs off of the Internet gave her a better glimpse of the anger and the messages within their songs. She enjoyed learning about this country and gets a kick out of asking people if they know where it is.

Photo Credits

AP/Wide World Photos: 58, 105 top, 133 bottom

Corbis Images: 102, 106 (AFP), 50 bottom (Archivo Iconografico S.A.), 48 (Bettmann), 72, 79, 87 (Bojan Brecelj), 126 (Ales Fevzer), 53 right (Hulton-Deutsch Collection), 95 (Reuters NewMedia Inc.), 18 (Janez Skok), 91, 132 top (Tim Thompson), 7 bottom, 42, 46, 54, 55, 56, 123 (Peter Turnley)

Corbis Sygma/Bojan Brecelj: 104

Getty Images: 103 (Donald Miralle), 59 (Keld Navntoft/STF/AFP)

ImageState/Roberto M. Arakaki: 7 top, 26

Mary Evans Picture Library: 94

Omni-Photo Communications/Amos Zezmer: 29, 90, 99, 131

Panos Pictures/IPA/www.ipak.com: 64, 82, 85, 88, 100, 108 bottom, 109, 110, 113, 116, 118, 122, 124, 125, 130 left (Bojan Brecelj), 47 (Dario Cortese), 15, 32, 39, 69, 132 bottom (Arne Hodalic), 25, 40 (Matja Kacicnik), 28 (Stane Klemenc), 62 (Borut Kranjc), 66 (Marko Modic),

105 bottom (Franc Oderlab), 34, 35, 36 (Hrvoje Ostanic), 68 (Borut Petrlin), 8, 23, 65 bottom (Janez Skok), 107 (Leon Stukelj), 2, 98, 101 (Gregory Wrona), 24 (Janez Zrnec)

Republic of Slovenia, Government Public Relations and Media Office/Kodia Photo & Graphis: 14, 96 (Ales Fevzer), 93 (Stojan Kerbler), 27 (Stane Klemenc), 76 (Kompas Archives), (Bojan Marceta), 41 (Ciril Mlinar), 11, 89, 115, 119 (Igor Modic), 57 right (Marko Pogacnik), 12, 97, 133 top (Zvone Seruga), 50 top (Marjan Smerke), 37, 108 top (Srdjan Zivulovic), 75 (Janez Zrnec), 60

Reuters/Srdjan Zivulovic: 86

Superstock, Inc.: 45 (Silvio Fiore), 78

Tim Thompson: 20, 22 bottom, 31, 44, 84, 120

TRIP Photo Library: 67, 71 bottom, 92, 112 (M Barlow), 70 (M Bartholomew), 74 (S Hill), 30 (G Ivory), 16 (M Jenkin), cover, 6 (N & J Wiseman), 83 (E Young)

Maps by XNR Productions